The School Health Service
1908 - 1974

Report of the
Chief Medical Officer of the
Department of Education and Science
and presenting an historical review
by Dr. Peter Henderson, Principal
Medical Officer of the Department
of Education and Science from 1951–1969

LONDON
HER MAJESTY'S STATIONERY OFFICE

ISBN 0 11 270409 3

CONTENTS

CONTENTS

THE SCHOOL HEALTH SERVICE
1908–1974

To the Secretary of State for Education and Science.

Sir,

INTRODUCTION

The year 1974 was a momentous one for the School Health Service in that, instead of being the responsibility of local education authorities, it was included in the National Health Service by the National Health Service Reorganisation Act 1973, which came into force on 1 April 1974. In these circumstances and to mark the end of an epoch, it was thought appropriate to review the school health service since its inception rather than to produce a traditional report on 'The Health of the School Child.'

Legislation affecting the health of school children was introduced as far back as 1906 and 1907. The basis for this legislation was the desire that ill health should not interfere with the learning process in schools. The emphasis was on prevention and detection and so successful was the latter that a considerable treatment element had to be developed. The 1907 legislation authorised local education authorities to provide their own treatment service and substantial progress in the health of school children followed.

It could reasonably have been expected that with the introduction of the National Health Service Act in 1946 the school health service, and particularly its treatment element, would have been included in the National Health Service. This was not done because it was considered that the welfare of school children was so important that a dual system, however illogical, was justified at that time. Twenty-five years later, however, the illogicality of a separate and independent school health service became more obvious. The foundations of the mental and physical health of children are laid in the pre-school years and more emphasis should be laid on the identification of deviation from normal development in the first 5 years of life and less reliance placed on periodic examinations of a captive population of children throughout school years.

A former tripartite system is to be unified, but how? Many school doctors feel they are being squeezed out of the system in order to perpetuate a bi-partite system supplied by consultant paediatricians and general practitioners. School doctors have special skills and knowledge and they may well ask: 'How many paediatricians or general practitioners have been inside a maintained school and what do they know about the medical component of learning problems?' The answer would have to be that a minority may know how schools and teachers operate but until such time as educational medicine is recognised as an integral part of paediatrics, there remains a very important role for doctors with additional training and experience to meet teachers, to support them in their

1

dealings with children with problems and to ensure that these children get the medical treatment and other remedial measures they need and that their parents receive helpful and consistent advice.

The period since the Report for 1971–72 has been characterised for the staff of the school health service by feelings of considerable anxiety about the future of this service and therefore also about their own future. It is to be hoped, however, that reorganisation of the National Health Service under the National Health Service Reorganisation Act 1973 will provide further opportunities for extending the benefit of the skills of those working in the school health service to children before they start school and for providing with consultant paediatricians and family doctors a unified health service for children of all ages. This health service will include preventive as well as curative and therapeutic aspects. These preventive aspects are not limited to protective action against infectious diseases but include identification of problems or potential problems at an early stage and taking steps to minimise the effect of these not only on the child himself but on his family. These steps include the mobilisation of all possible sources of help to a family, or child with a problem, and to his teachers, including counselling, remedial and special education and social support of all kinds. This kind of preventive support is always difficult to quantify and to cost and it is always at a disadvantage in competition with traditional more glamorous curative medicine.

The role and training of the school physician were authoritatively defined for the USA by Milton Senn in 1965*. He said that the school system needed the school physician and that every school should have a doctor trained in both medical and behavioural sciences. This he considered was a job that should not be viewed as a part-time supplementary position but as a separate chosen professional field of work with children in their years of greatest development. Ideally it was considered that such a doctor would receive post-graduate training in paediatrics, child growth and personality development, public health, educational philosophy and community organisation. Although this country lags behind the USA in that school doctors have not yet attained the professional recognition implicit in Dr. Senn's definition, many of them have specialist training and knowledge of educational medicine and are able to provide an integrated service involving children, parents, teachers and medical colleagues.

The Committee reviewing Child Health Services under the chairmanship of Professor Court, is considering how health services for children may best be organised in a unified service and it seems likely that members of the committee will be well aware of the special contribution school doctors and nurses and other professional staff have made towards the improved health of the nation's children for more than 60 years, and they will be aware, too, of the need for continuation and development of this contribution and for its extension to all children.

The historical review of the school health service 1908 to 1974 is the work of Dr. Peter Henderson who retired in 1969 after 18 years as Principal Medical Officer to the Department of Education and Science. As Sir George Godber wrote of him in the Introduction to 'The Health of the School Child 1966–68': 'In the years since the Medical Department of the then Board of Education was

---

* Paediatric Clinics of North America. 12, 1039.

established no one had rendered it greater service than Dr. Henderson.' The review is yet another example of this informed and devoted service.

The section on the School Dental Service was contributed by the dental staff of the Department of Health and Social Security.

The statistics included in the Appendices to this Report relate to 1973, the last full year of the school health service as an independent agency. In future, these statistics will be divided between DHSS and DES publications. Reports relevant to the health of school children will be included in the child health section of the Chief Medical Officer's Annual Report 'On the State of the Public Health' while future reports relating to the special education of handicapped children will be published from time to time by the Department of Education and Science.

I am, Sir,

Your obedient servant,

Henry Yellowlees.

3

THE SCHOOL HEALTH SERVICE
1908-1974

As in so many fields of human endeavour provision for the health and education of this country's children was first made by the pioneering efforts of private individuals, singly or in association, and often against scepticism or outright opposition. In general, health and education services developed in parallel, particularly the school health and education services for handicapped children.

Statutory Developments

Although hospitals and schools had been established in earlier centuries, and mainly by religious organizations, it was not until the nineteenth century that the State first assumed some responsibility for the education and health of children.

In 1807 an Education Bill to provide elementary education for all children was rejected by Parliament; but, in 1833 the Government, for the first time, made a grant of £20,000 to voluntary organizations to help them build 'schoolhouses for the children of the poorer classes.' In 1839 the grant was increased to £30,000; a Committee of the Privy Council on Education was appointed with a permanent secretary and an inspectorate to administer these annual grants. This Committee became the Education Department in 1856, the Board of Education in 1900, the Ministry of Education in 1945, and the Department of Education and Science in 1964.

In 1833, also, a Factory Act was passed that prohibited children under 11 years of age from working more than 9 hours a day. And it was in 1833 that deaths from the cholera epidemic that broke out in 1831 reached a total of almost 50,000, causing widespread alarm and increased public pressure on the Government to institute sanitary reforms. It was not until 1847 that the first medical officer of health was appointed—in Liverpool; the second was in London in 1848. In 1848, also, the first Public Health Act was passed by Parliament and the General Board of Health established that became the Local Government Board in 1871, the Ministry of Health in 1919, and the Department of Health and Social Security in 1968.

In 1870, when only about half of the children of elementary school age attended school, many of them being indifferently taught, Parliament passed the Elementary Education Act that provided for the election of school boards with the power to build and maintain schools in areas without church schools. When introducing this Education Bill, W. E. Forster, MP for Bradford, said that it was his 'conviction that the education rate would never exceed three pence' (Wallas, 1940); 100 years later, in 1969-70, public expenditure on education in Great Britain amounted to £2,346 million. Elementary education was made compulsory in 1880 and free in 1891. Between 1870 and 1890 the school population increased from $1\frac{1}{4}$ million to $4\frac{1}{2}$ million children.

The State was equally slow in providing or arranging education for handicapped children. So far as is known the first school in Britain to accept a handicapped pupil was Thomas Braidwood's school in Edinburgh for teaching mathematics; a deaf boy was admitted to it in 1760—the same year that the Abbé de l'Epée established in Paris the National Institute for Deaf Mutes; this was the first school to be opened in any country for the handicapped children of the poor.

In 1791 the School of Instruction for the Indigent Blind, the first in Britain, was started in Liverpool with many of the pupils blind from smallpox; 7 years later Jenner, a medical practitioner in Gloucestershire, proved conclusively that smallpox could be prevented by vaccination. It was not until 1971 that the routine vaccination of children against smallpox was no longer officially thought to be necessary in the United Kingdom (Department of Health and Social Security, 1971).

It took the State 100 years from the opening of this voluntary school in Liverpool to make statutory provision for handicapped children. In 1893 the Elementary Education (Blind and Deaf Children) Act, and in 1899 the Elementary Education (Defective and Epileptic Children) Act were passed by Parliament. In the intervening years other schools for handicapped children had been opened by voluntary organizations and school boards.

Compulsory and free elementary education brought millions of children to school and quickly produced incontrovertible evidence that many of them were in such poor health that their education was adversely affected.

As early as 1812 Dr. James Ware reported on the eyesight of London children and Oxford students. In 1880 Dr. Priestley Smith, in a paper on 'Short Sight in relation to Education', gave the results of his examination of the eyes of 2,000 school children and training college students in Birmingham. In 1882 Dr. Clement Dykes, medical officer at Rugby School, published a book on 'Health at School'. And in 1884 Dr. (later Sir) J. Crichton Browne wrote a report for the Education Department on what he considered to be 'mental overpressure' in the public elementary schools of London (Board of Education, 1910a).

On the Continent of Europe influential doctors were also urging their governments to provide for the health of school children. In 1840 school doctors were appointed to some teacher training colleges in Sweden. In 1883 the eminent ophthalmologist, Dr. Cohn of Breslau, strongly advocated the appointment of school doctors; it was in that year that the first one was appointed in Germany— in Frankfurt-am-Main. In 1885 the first school doctor in Switzerland was appointed in Lausanne. By 1890 the medical inspection of school children had been organized in all the departments of France.

In Britain the London School Board, in 1890, was the first to appoint a school doctor; the second was the Bradford Board in 1893. By 1905 school doctors had been appointed by 85 local education authorities and medical inspection of school children was being carried out in 48 areas. About 300 special schools with 17,000 handicapped children had also been established.

The reports of these school doctors on the amount of ill-health, malnutrition, and disability among school children were reinforced by the highly critical authoritative Reports from a Royal Commission and two Interdepartmental

5

Committees (Royal Commission on Physical Training in Scotland, 1903; Interdepartmental Committee on Physical Deterioration, 1904; Interdepartmental Committee on Medical Inspection and Feeding of Children attending Public Elementary Schools, 1905).

Following the publication of these three Reports the Government decided that a School Medical Service (renamed School Health Service in 1945) should be organized on a national basis and that local education authorities should be empowered to provide, or to assist voluntary school canteen committees to provide, meals for children attending elementary schools who were unable to take full advantage of the education provided owing to lack of food. In 1906 the Education (Provision of Meals) Act, and in 1907 the Education (Administrative Provisions) Act were passed by Parliament.

The latter Act gave local education authorities the duty to provide for the medical inspection of children in public elementary schools and the power to make arrangements, with the sanction of the Board of Education, for attending to their health and physical condition. In 1907 a Medical Branch (renamed Special Services Branch in 1945 and Medical Services Branch in 1972) was formed in the Board of Education. Later that year Circular 576 (probably the most influential in the history of the service) was sent to local education authorities giving them general guidance on the aims of the school medical service. The circular stated that '. . . the work of medical inspection should be carried out in intimate conjunction with the Public Health Authorities and under the direct supervision of the Medical Officer of Health. . . . One of the objects of the new legislation is to stimulate a sense of duty in matters affecting health in the homes of the people, to enlist the best services and interests of parents. . . . It is in the home, in fact, that both the seed and the fruit of public health are to be found.'

Further guidance on the conduct of the school medical service was given in Circulars 582 and 596 issued by the Board of Education in 1908.

Circular 582 advised local education authorities that the medical inspection of each child should on average take no more than 'a few minutes'; the children as a rule need only have their clothes 'loosened or be partially undressed'; 'needless medical examination of healthy children should, for obvious reasons, be avoided'; 'the vision of children under six years of age should not be tested'; and tests of hearing should be applied 'only in a general way' (the compulsory age for starting school was 5 years for all children except those who were deaf for whom 7 years of age was then thought to be early enough; it was not until 1938 that the age was reduced to 5 years for deaf children).

Circular 596 discussed, among other subjects, the provision of school clinics for the treatment of children with defects found at school medical inspections. Before the Board of Education would sanction a school clinic it had to be satisfied that '. . . only those children shall be treated in a school clinic for whose treatment adequate provision cannot otherwise be made, whether by the parents or by voluntary associations or institutions, such as hospitals, or through the agency of the Poor Law.' The first school clinic in this country was opened in Bradford, in 1908.

Regulations made under the Education Act of 1918 gave local education authorities the duty (previously they had only the power) to make arrangements

6

for the treatment of children attending public elementary schools, and for the medical inspection of children in secondary schools; they were also given the power, not the duty, to arrange for the treatment of children in secondary schools.

In 1919, the Ministry of Health Act established the Ministry of Health 'to promote the health of the people.' This Act transferred to the Minister of Health all the powers and duties of the Board of Education for the medical inspection and treatment of children and young persons, with the proviso that these powers and duties might by arrangement be exercised by the Board of Education on behalf of the Minister of Health. The proviso was, in fact, adopted and the Chief Medical Officer of the Ministry of Health became also Chief Medical Officer of the Board of Education and of its successors—first the Ministry of Education and then the Department of Education and Science.

Although the development of the school health service was seriously inter-rupted by the two World Wars it expanded rapidly after each of them, particularly after the War of 1939–1945. The Education Act of 1944, gave local education authorities the duty to provide school meals and milk for pupils at schools maintained by them; the duty to provide medical and dental inspection in all types of maintained primary and secondary schools; and the duty to provide or secure for children attending maintained schools all forms of medical and dental treatment, other than domiciliary treatment, without cost to the parents. The National Health Service Act of 1946, that came into force in 1948, enabled local education authorities to make arrangements with regional hospital boards and the Governors of Teaching Hospitals for free specialist and hospital treatment for children attending maintained schools.

From the outset, but even more so during the last 25 years, the school health service has been specially concerned with handicapped children, particularly those with behaviour and emotional difficulties, epilepsy, mental retardation, visual defects, defective hearing, speech and language disorders, and physical disabilities. And all through the years it gave sympathetic attention to children from socially deprived homes—by recommending free school meals and milk, admission to convalescent homes or to day and boarding special schools for delicate children.

In recent years there has been much questioning of the value of periodic medical examination of all children at school, other than the routine medical examination of children when they first start school. The Ministry of Education amended its Regulations in 1953, and again in 1959, to give local education authorities more freedom of choice in arranging school medical examinations. As a result more selective methods of choosing children for these examinations have been adopted by many school doctors but there is no single or easy way of doing this. The aim is to concentrate the skill and experience of school doctors on children in need of medical investigation, treatment, and supervision.

From increasing experience of the working of the National Health Service it became generally accepted that the three main branches of the service—General Practitioner, Hospital and Specialist, and Local Authority Health Services—including the school health service—should be reorganised to form a unified, comprehensive national service. The National Health Service Reorganization Act of 1973, that came into force on 1 April 1974, brought the three branches

7

together and transferred the statutory responsibility for providing school health services from the local education authorities to the Secretary of State for Social Services. This Act gives the Secretary of State the duty to provide medical and dental inspection and treatment for pupils attending local education authority schools, and the power to do so for junior and senior pupils at any non-maintained educational establishment by arrangement with the proprietor or for pupils who receive education otherwise than at school. The Act also gives the Secretary of State powers to provide, by arrangement with any local education authority, medical and dental inspection or treatment of senior pupils attending any maintained educational establishment, other than a school, at which full-time further education is provided. Local education authorities and the managers or governors of voluntary schools have the duty to make available to the Secretary of State for Social Services such accommodation as is appropriate for the carrying out of health services in their schools.

The National Health Service Reorganization Act of 1973 brought to a close the long and honourable record of achievement of the central and local education authorities in providing for the health of children at school. The full support of these authorities, however, and of the teachers must be retained if the school health service is to continue to be vigorous and progressive under its new administration. The need for this close working relationship was stressed in the White Paper on National Health Service Reorganisation that was presented to Parliament in August, 1972, by the Secretary of State for Social Services: 'Those providing health services for school children will need to work closely with the hospital service and personal health services for families and children and with the education service. . . . There will be arrangements for joint planning and co-ordination of the two services.'

These aims will not be achieved unless there is continuing joint discussion and reassessment of needs and provision all the way along, and not at the outset only, by the health and education services, centrally and locally. And, of crucial importance, a school health service to be worth the name must be centred on the schools, not hospitals, with the teachers, medical and medical ancillary staff as partners in a joint enterprise with the parents. The Working Party on Collaboration between the National Health Service and Local Government (Department of Health and Social Security, 1973a) stated specifically that local education authorities and teachers were concerned that the value of the school health service 'shall be fully recognised and sufficient resources devoted to it, and also that the medical and other staff shall continue to see themselves as part of the team responsible with the education service for trying to provide the best opportunity for each individual child.'

Development of School Clinic Provision

In the early days of the school medical service it was quickly realised that existing medical facilities for the general population were inadequate to deal with the mass of defects found in children at school medical inspections. There was, however, much opposition to local education authorities providing treatment for these children. Even such a distinguished and sympathetic school medical officer as Dr. James Kerr of London (who prior to his appointment in London in 1902 had been school medical officer in Bradford from 1893) was of the opinion that 'to treat the ailment discovered would tend to pauperise the parent' (Report of the Interdepartmental Committee on Medical Inspection and Feeding of Children attending Public Elementary Schools, 1905).

Before a local education authority could provide a school clinic it had to obtain the sanction of the Board of Education that, at first, applied rigorous constraints. Yet, only two years after the Board first issued advice on the scope of school clinics its Chief Medical Officer, Dr. (later Sir) George Newman, in his Annual Report for 1910, said that a school clinic had two main functions: it was a centre for 'inspection' and a centre for 'treatment'; he discussed these functions in considerable detail.

An *inspection clinic* allowed more time than was available at school medical inspections for the thorough examination of children thought to require investigation, particularly 'chest cases', and those with impaired hearing or vision, or suspected to be 'mentally defective'. Such a clinic provided a convenient centre for co-ordinating the agencies used for following up children requiring treatment or supervision: 'From it should be directed and organized the work of the school medical officer, school nurse, attendance officer and care committee. . . . The teacher will find the clinic invaluable. . . . And, lastly, the parent will be glad occasionally to make use of it . . . in regard to one or other of the various matters affecting a child's school life.'

The team concept of health supervision of school children that is now so much spoken about had, in fact, already been formed in the Medical Branch of the Board of Education almost 70 years ago. But, due, perhaps, to the limited responsibilities and training given to attendance officers, later termed school welfare officers, full use was not everywhere made of their potential. Also, few local education authorities thought it necessary to adopt the much publicised school care committee system of the London Education Authority.

From the start the working partnership between school doctor and school nurse was close and has remained so ever since. In practice, the school nurse has been a medical-social worker; visiting homes to advise mothers on the care and treatment of their children has been an essential part of her duties. In the poorer districts this was difficult, up-hill work, but in the end, and in co-operation with the teachers, it has had its reward in better-fed, better-clad and, in general, better-cared for children. The work of the school nurse, whether a qualified health visitor or not, has always had a large content of health education of a most practical kind.

As the years passed the scope of the inspection clinic widened until it became an assessment as well as a diagnostic centre, with the parents, usually the mothers, invited to be present at the examination of their children. Increasingly, and particularly in urban areas, other professional workers were employed, including audiologists, audiometricians, chiropodists, orthoptists, physiotherapists, and speech therapists, and the links between the school health and the school psychological services, were strengthened.

The *treatment clinic* was intended to be organized according to the types of diseases and defects treated. The simplest form was that for the treatment of minor ailments, particularly certain diseases of the skin and eyes that were prevalent in the early days of the service. Such treatment was considered to be the responsibility of the school nurse, supervised by the school doctor. Other clinics would provide a more extensive service, including treatment of diseases of the ears, X-ray treatment of ringworm of the scalp, dental treatment, the provision of spectacles, and, where alternative facilities were not available, operative treatment of tonsils and adenoids in school clinic premises or in hospitals.

Most local education authorities, however, were reluctant to provide an operating theatre for tonsillectomy in their clinics, and, in time, were discouraged from doing so by the Board of Education. The number of education authorities providing facilities for, or paying for, a tonsillectomy service increased from 2 in 1910 to 111 in 1922; thereafter, the authorities concerned gradually stopped this particular service so that by 1938 only about 50 continued to provide it; shortly after the Second World War this tonsillectomy service came to an end, Nottingham being the last education authority to discontinue tonsillectomy operations in a school clinic. Despite greatly improved child health and the introduction of sulpha drugs, penicillin and other antibiotics, every year in this country over 100,000 school children undergo tonsillectomy. The need for subjecting so many children to this operation has often been questioned—not least in successive issues of 'The Health of the School Child'.

From the start of the service particular attention was paid to children with rheumatism and rheumatic heart disease. The need for action by local education and health authorities was mentioned in several of the early reports of the Chief Medical Officer of the Board of Education. In his report for 1926 he stressed the need for, among other provisions, the setting up of 'a rheumatism centre or cardiac consultation clinic . . . at the local hospital, school clinic or elsewhere' (Board of Education 1927a). By 1932, the London County Council's arrangements for the diagnosis and treatment of children with rheumatism and rheumatic heart disease, including 16 rheumatism supervisory centres, were the most comprehensive in this country. Other local education authorities had also established clinics for children with rheumatic heart disease, and their number continued to increase up to the outbreak of the Second World War. Since then there has been a dramatic reduction in the number of children with chronic rheumatic heart disease and local education authorities no longer provide clinics for them.

The expansion of school clinic provision has been a notable feature of the development of the school health service in this country. About 30 clinic premises were in operation by 1910; their number increased to 350 by 1914 to 692 by 1919 and to about 2,853 by 1972.

With the passing of the years the school clinic became an increasingly important part of the work of the school health service; the distinction formerly drawn between 'inspection' and 'treatment' clinics became blurred, the functions of the one having merged with those of the other. Prior to the National Health Service, the school clinic was for many school children the only 'paediatric' clinic in their area. Special sessions for children with conditions such as asthma, bed-wetting, and malnutrition were started by school doctors particularly interested in these conditions: by 1971 special sessions for asthmatic children were being held in over 60 school clinics and for bed-wetters in about 230 clinics.

Although most of the defects first found at school medical examinations are comparatively minor, some are serious and many would worsen if they remained

10

untreated. About half of these defects were not being treated when first detected by the school health service (Department of Health and Social Security, 1973b).

Almost from the beginning of the school health service consultants from the hospital service were employed on a sessional basis by some local education authorities; their number increased until by 1938 over 400 ophthalmic surgeons, 200 ear, nose and throat surgeons, and 150 orthopaedic surgeons were working in school clinics and paid by local education authorities. In the period between the coming into force of the Education Act, 1944, and the National Health Service Act, 1946, local education authorities had to arrange, or themselves bear the cost of, free medical and surgical treatment, other than domiciliary treatment, for children attending their schools. When the National Health Service became responsible, in July 1948, for hospital and specialist treatment many of the consultants previously employed part-time by local education authorities continued to work in school clinics although employed and paid by the National Health Service; by 1971, about 300 ophthalmic surgeons, 250 psychiatrists, and 200 other consultants were employed part-time, and 14 psychiatrists full-time, in the school health service but paid by the National Health Service; in addition, local education authorities employed about 90 part-time and 19 full-time psychiatrists.

These specialist services in school clinics are of the greatest value to school children, their parents, and teachers; they provide early treatment and continuing specialist supervision in an unhurried environment; they reduce the volume of work that would otherwise have to be provided for in busy and often over-crowded hospital out-patient departments which may be at a long distance from the children's homes and schools; and they bring the hospital consultant and school doctor into a close working relationship to their mutual benefit.

The School Nursing Service

The school nursing service has been, and continues to be, a vital part of the school health service. Much of the nurses' work was done in the homes of the children, particularly socially deprived homes; and much of this work was health education of a very practical kind. Many mothers relied on the school nurses and sought their advice when they hesitated to approach doctors or teachers. The school nurses have been the chief link between home, school and school clinic. Some were employed wholly or mainly in school clinics or special schools but most were engaged in the full range of school nursing duties. They accompanied school doctors at the medical examinations of children in schools. It was their duty to see that children found in need of treatment obtained it: in the early days this often entailed frequent home visits to persuade parents to have their children treated. They visited the schools in their area regularly and discussed with the teachers children whose health or general condition caused concern. They carried out screening tests of hearing and vision, and were responsible for the cleanliness inspections of children in school. As the years passed and the health and general condition of the children improved, with fewer requiring treatment at minor ailments clinics, the school nurses became more involved in the early ascertainment and supervision of handicapped children, in those with personal problems, and in health education.

More of them combined school health with maternity and child welfare work. The Handicapped Pupils and School Health Service Regulations, 1945, prescribed

11

that in future all school nurses (except existing school nurses and those employed solely in school clinics, in boarding special schools, or on specialist duties) should be qualified health visitors. In fact, many of them already had this qualification and had for years been family health visitors and not concerned only with school children. Since 1945 the co-ordination of school and maternity and child welfare nursing services has become the general pattern of organisation throughout the country. In recent years health visitors have, increasingly, become 'attached' part-time to the practices of general medical practitioners.

Whether as a 'top nurse manager' or a 'first line nurse manager' or a 'middle nurse manager', or however designated in current nurse management jargon, the school nursing service will always need women of the character and capability of the majority of those who served as school nurses in the years between 1908 and 1974, and who did so much for the children, their parents, and their teachers.

Staffing of the School Health Service other than the School Dental Staff

School Doctors

Only a small minority of school doctors have, at any period, worked full-time in the school health service; the majority have also done other medical work, most of them in the local health authority services. Latterly, an increasing number have been general practitioners, or doctors in other branches of medicine, or married women doctors. In 1972, of the 3,400 school doctors in England and Wales only about 120 worked full-time in the school health service; about 1,900 also worked in the local health authority services; about 800 were general practitioners and about 500 worked in other branches of medicine, were married women doctors, or had retired from other medical work. In total, the time these various doctors gave to the school health service amounted to the equivalent of 1,060 full-time doctors, serving a school population of about 8½ million.

School Nurses

In 1972 about 10,000 nurses worked in the school health service in England and Wales; 6,900 had the health visitor's certificate; in total, the time they gave to the school health service amounted to the equivalent of 3,370 full-time nurses.

An increasing number of local education authorities employ assistants without professional nurse-training to help school nurses with their less skilled work; 736 nurses' assistants were employed in 1972 of whom over 300 were full-time and over 400 part-time.

Other Professional Staff

In recent years not only have more school doctors, nurses and consultants been engaged in the school health service but also an increasing number of workers in professions allied to medicine. By 1972 the service employed about 430 full-time and 500 part-time speech therapists, 263 full-time and 172 part-time qualified social workers, about 40 full-time and 40 part-time other social workers, 150 full-time and 260 part-time physiotherapists, 60 full-time and 180 part-time chiropodists, 80 full-time and 110 part-time audiometricians, 14 full-time and 50 part-time orthoptists, and 30 full-time and 80 part-time psycho-

12

therapists. Of the 700 educational psychologists employed by local education authorities about 300 worked in the child guidance clinics of the school health service, and 400 in the school psychological service.

Handicapped Children

In 1972 over 100,000 handicapped boys and girls were being taught in special schools, in special classes in ordinary schools, in hospitals, in their homes, or in independent schools through arrangements made by local education authorities. In addition, about 15,000 were on the waiting lists for special schools. A much larger number were in ordinary schools including many with physical disabilities, emotional and behaviour problems, speech and language disorders, and educational retardation, as well as many from socially deprived homes.

Over the years there has been increasing pressure not only from parents of handicapped children but also from some doctors, teachers, social workers and others for handicapped boys and girls to be taught in ordinary schools. In 1954, the Ministry of Education, in Circular 276, stated that official policy was: 'no handicapped pupil should be sent to a special school who can be satisfactorily educated in an ordinary school. Where a special school is necessary a day school is preferable if it offers a satisfactory and practicable solution.'

Apart from blind, partially-sighted, and deaf children, almost all of whom are taught in special schools, more children in the other educational categories of handicap attend ordinary than special schools. In 1970, about 90,000 school children were treated in speech therapy clinics but fewer than 400 were in special schools on account of speech and language disorders; about 70,000 maladjusted school children were treated in child guidance clinics but less than 10,000 were in special schools; almost 10,000 boys and girls with epilepsy were medically examined in ordinary schools but only 800 were in special schools; over 10,000 physically handicapped children were known to be in ordinary schools and 9,000 in special schools (Department of Education and Science, 1972*b*).

In general, children who are severely affected are in special schools but there are many exceptions, particularly among the physically handicapped. In 1970, for example, about 1,500 boys and girls with spina bifida were in special schools in England; 800 were in ordinary schools of whom 300 were incontinent, 300 required a walking aid, 150 were in wheel chairs, and 120 had a Spitz-Holter valve (Department of Education and Science, 1972*c*). Many of these 800 boys and girls were as severely handicapped as the 1,500 in special schools.

Another indication of the trend towards educating handicapped children in ordinary schools has been the provision of special classes in ordinary schools; by 1972 about 5,000 children, most of whom were either partially-hearing or maladjusted, were being taught in such classes. Systematic experiments in the education of visually handicapped children either in ordinary or special classes in ordinary schools were recently recommended (Department of Education and Science, 1972*d*).

Visually Handicapped Children

Although almost half a million children with eye conditions are dealt with annually by the school health service only a small minority are visually handicapped and require special education. In 1971 about 1,100 were in special

13

schools for the blind and 2,000 in special schools and classes for the partially-sighted. In 1920, when the school population was much smaller, 2,700 blind children were in special schools.

In 1948 there was a sudden increase in the number of blind and severely partially-sighted babies that continued until about 1955. Some other countries had a similar experience. The babies were all premature and of small birth weight. It was found that the amount of oxygen given to them to save their lives caused fibrotic changes in their eyes behind the lens, a condition termed retro-lental fibroplasia. Preventive measures taken after this catastrophe dramatically reduced the number of babies developing the condition.

The reduction in the number of blind children has been due largely to the control and early treatment of communicable diseases that once caused blindness. Better and widespread ante-natal care of mothers, and preventive treatment of the eyes of new-born babies, have practically eliminated gonoccocal infection of the eyes of babies that was once one of the chief causes of blindness.

Blindness from congenital syphilis is now also rare; in 1971 only 16 infants were treated for this disease in all the National Health Service venereal disease clinics in England and Wales.

German Measles (rubella) if contracted by a woman in the early months of pregnancy may damage the eyes, ears, heart, and brain of the developing foetus. Vaccination of school girls against rubella was introduced in 1970; if persisted with, and if successful, the number of babies with congenital defects from rubella should be reduced substantially.

A survey in 1968 found that 215 visually handicapped children under 6 years of age in England and Wales were also deaf or partially-hearing: 46 were blind and deaf, 30 were blind and partially-hearing, 49 were deaf and partially-sighted, and 90 were partially-sighted and partially-hearing (Department of Education and Science, 1969b).

About 8 per cent of boys and 0·5 per cent of girls have difficulty in distinguishing certain colours, mainly red and green, and, in consequence, some employments are barred to them. In practically every area the school health service gives colour discrimination tests to children before they leave school, usually at about 11 years of age; in some areas boys only are tested.

It has been estimated that about 4 per cent of 6-year-old children squint (Adelstein and Scully, 1967). Usually, the condition is first observed and treatment started in infancy; sometimes, however, it is first dealt with only when the child starts school and comes under the supervision of the school health service. If uncorrected a squinting eye may, by about the age of 8 years, become functionally blind.

In almost every area children have their vision tested by the school health service shortly after they first start school; this should be the practice everywhere. In some areas the school health service does annual vision screening of all children.

A survey in 1962–1965 of children in special schools and classes for the blind and partially-sighted found that over half of the blind and rather less than half

14

of the partially-sighted children also had emotional, intellectual, physical or speech and language disorders (Fine, S. R., 1968).

The school health service has a vital part in the selection of children for special schools and classes for the partially-sighted. The children are not classified as partially-sighted on the results of visual acuity tests alone: a child's intelligence, personality, quality of parental support and encouragement, as well as the rate of progress in ordinary school are taken into account. There are children who make satisfactory progress in ordinary schools who are as severely visually handicapped as those in special schools and classes for the partially-sighted. Satisfactory school placement is achieved only if there is full and joint assessment of a child's disabilities, attainments, and potentialities by the school health service, including an ophthalmologist, the teachers, and the school psychological service.

Hearing Handicapped Children

Children with defective hearing have been of particular concern to the school health service ever since it started. The first Annual Report of the Chief Medical Officer of the Board of Education, for the year 1908, said that: 'It is not usually practical during the routine examination of large numbers of children to test accurately the exact condition of the hearing capacity of a child, and, indeed, such a procedure can hardly be said to be necessary.' He went on to say, however, that 'It is important that a careful examination should be made of all children in whom there is any reason to suspect defective hearing.' He was also of the opinion that 'about one quarter' of deaf pupils 'will fail to learn by the oral method, especially among the congenital deaf mutes and among the feeble-minded deaf. . . . For children who are incapable of speech, finger spelling and written language must be the principal media of instruction' (Board of Education, 1910*b*).

Two years later the Chief Medical Officer wrote: 'Among the requirements of a satisfactory scheme of medical inspection is that of applying a hearing test to every child who is old enough to respond' (Board of Education, 1911).

At that time there were 48 schools for the deaf attended by 3,500 children. There were also separate classes for partially deaf children in three schools for the deaf.

In his Report for 1919 the Chief Medical Officer urged the need for early ascertainment and early school attendance: 'from the age of two to the age of seven attendance is optional and only becomes compulsory at seven. The disadvantages of this statutory provision are considerable and Authorities are not as a rule willing to incur the heavy expenditure of special education so long as the law does not compel them to do so, and the deaf child is involved in serious educational loss in consequence. The early beginnings of speech which come more easy to the young child are withheld from him until a later age, and it may safely be said that the majority of deaf children never make up for the loss sustained by postponing the beginning of education until seven or, as often happens, till later. It is desirable, therefore, pending an alteration in the statute that Education Authorities should understand for themselves the importance of sending deaf children to school at an early age' (Board of Education, 1920).

15

In 1927 it was suggested that deaf children might be classified in four categories: deaf mutes, deaf semi-mutes, speaking deaf, and the partially deaf, the first three groups being taught in special schools for the deaf, and the fourth in a school or class for the partially deaf, or in the front seats of an ordinary class in an ordinary school (Board of Education, 1928a).

The imperfections of the methods used before the introduction of audiometry to detect 'partial deafness', particularly the 'whispered voice' test, were mentioned in 'The Health of the School Child' for 1930 with the comment: 'The need for some more scientific method has now been met by the introduction of the audiometer' (Board of Education, 1931a). At that time a gramophone audiometer was being used by the school health service in Birmingham, London, and Tottenham.

By 1931 over 1,700 partially-deaf children had been ascertained by school doctors, and over 200 of them were in special schools for the partially deaf in Birmingham, Bradford, Bristol and London (Board of Education, 1932).

A 'Study of the Deaf in England and Wales' by Dr. Alfred Eichholz, a former Chief Medical Inspector of the Board of Education, was published in 1932. This was a penetrating, comprehensive review of the subject and one that had much influence among school doctors, teachers, and administrators. It led to the appointment, in 1934, of a Committee of Inquiry into 'The Medical, Educational, and Social Aspects of the Problems attending children suffering from Defect of Hearing not amounting to Total Deafness.' The Committee's Report was published in 1938 (Board of Education, 1938). It recommended that there should be four grades (three main grades with grade 2 having two subdivisions) of children with defective hearing based on the type of education they needed instead of on degree of hearing loss. Other recommendations included: the school medical service of every local education authority should have arrangements for the treatment of ear disease and defective hearing; there should be routine group testing with a gramophone audiometer of the hearing of all children in ordinary schools; and that day special classes for partially-hearing children should be established in schools for the deaf, not in ordinary schools. Consideration of these recommendations were interrupted by the Second World War.

The Education Act of 1944 gave local education authorities the duty of ascertaining handicapped children, including those with defective hearing, from the age of 2 years, and the power to provide special education for those aged 2–5 years and the duty to do so for those aged 5–16 years.

In the early 1940s Professor and Mrs. Irene Ewing, at Manchester University, and Miss Edith Whetnall, FRCS, in London, were urging the need for diagnosis of defective hearing well before the age of 2 years, and for the instruction of parents of deaf infants and young children in the technique of auditory training so that they could train their young deaf child to listen to speech and other sounds all through their waking hours. Clinics for the training of parents were established in Manchester and London, and Professor and Mrs. Ewing also started short courses for health visitors on the use of simple hearing tests with infants and very young children.

16

At about that time pure-tone audiometry was replacing gramophone audiometry. The introduction of the Medresco hearing aid, free of charge through the National Health Service, was another important development.

In 1948, a teacher of the deaf was appointed to the Royal National Throat, Nose and Ear Hospital in Golden Square, London. This was the beginning of the peripatetic teacher service for hearing handicapped children that now employs over 150 teachers of the deaf; they help in the ascertainment of deaf and partially-hearing children, in parent guidance, and visit ordinary schools to advise teachers with partially-hearing children in their classes; they work closely with the school health service, with the special schools and classes, and with the youth employment service. In addition, over 170 teachers of the deaf are employed in special classes in ordinary schools for partially-hearing children; and about a score work in the audiology clinics of the school health service.

Until 1966 when Larchmoor School, Stoke Poges, Buckinghamshire, was opened by the Royal National Institute for the Deaf, for maladjusted deaf children there were no facilities in this country for the treatment of maladjusted deaf boys and girls.

Although there are now elaborate school health and special educational arrangements for deaf and partially-hearing children much still remains to be done for them. By 1967, the school health service had arranged for the routine audiometric testing of all school entrants in only 86 of the 162 local education authority areas; in two areas some entrants were tested; in 44 areas routine testing of all children was postponed to the ages of 6–8 years; and in the remaining 24 areas individual children only were tested when this was thought necessary. The need for a comprehensive audiological service for children including better arrangements for the maintenance of individual and group hearing aids in special schools and classes, and for the regular re-calibration of audiometers, has recently been urged (Reed, M. 1971).

As a result of early diagnosis, auditory training, early education, and technological advances many children who, in the early years of the school health service, would have been regarded, and taught, as deaf are now taught as partially-hearing. This has been sheer gain. Unfortunately, pre-lingually deaf children have not fared so well. A survey of 359 deaf pupils, aged 15–16 years, in 36 schools for the deaf in England and Wales, in 1962–1963, found that only 22 per cent of them had intelligible speech, 23 per cent had unintelligible speech, and 55 per cent had speech that ranged from the almost unintelligible to intelligible with difficulty. The same investigator did a more restricted survey of 167 fifteen-year old children in 20 schools for the deaf, in 1969–1970; she found that 39 per cent had intelligible speech and 16 per cent (21 per cent if grammar school pupils were omitted) unintelligible speech (Department of Education and Science, 1964 and 1972e). A recent Report stated that 15–16 year old deaf children had a mean reading age of only 7·8 years (Redgate, Palmer, Wilkins, Smart and Black, 1972).

In 1964, the Secretary of State for Education and Science appointed a Committee to consider the possible place of finger-spelling and signing in the education of deaf children. The Committee reported that 'The view that there is a place for manual media for some deaf children was supported in the evidence of all our witnesses', and recommended that 'research studies should be under-

17

taken to determine whether or not and in what circumstances the introduction of manual media of communication would lead to improvement in the education of deaf children' (Department of Education and Science, 1968a).

Manual means of communication are now being used in some special schools, mainly with deaf children with additional handicaps. A few teachers and speech therapists are also using the Paget-Gorman Sign System as an aid to teach young children who are deaf, deaf and partially-sighted, or aphasic.

Thus, it would appear that the educational difficulties of deaf children are not very different from what they were in 1908 when the Chief Medical Officer of the Board of Education was of the opinion that about a quarter of deaf pupils were likely to fail to learn by the oral method only.

Children with Speech and Language Disorders

Manchester was the first local education authority in this country to arrange for the treatment of children with speech defects when, in 1906, it started classes for school children who stammered. In the next two years similar classes were started in several Lancashire towns, and in Oxford and Gillingham in the south of England (Board of Education, 1914a).

The speech therapy service developed slowly; by 1926 a few education authorities had arranged for their teachers who held classes for stammerers to give speech training to children with cleft palate (Board of Education, 1927). In 1932 it was suggested that students in teacher training colleges should receive instruction in speech training and on speech defects (Board of Education, 1933). In the following year the Association of Education Committees adopted a resolution, submitted by the Stockton-on-Tees Education Committee, that the Government should be pressed to make it a duty of local education authorities to provide treatment for school children with defective speech. This duty was, in fact, imposed on local education authorities by the Education Act of 1944; and speech defect was included as one of the educational categories of handicap in the Handicapped Pupils and School Health Service Regulations, 1945.

It was not until 1945, following the founding of the College of Speech Therapists, that a common syllabus of training and examination were adopted for all speech therapy students. The training of speech therapists in England was first started at the Central School of Speech and Drama in London, in association with St. Thomas' Hospital, in 1919; about 1925 the training of speech therapists was introduced at the West End Hospital for Nervous Diseases, London, where a School of Speech Therapy was established in 1929. The establishment of other training schools followed and by 1967 there were 9 in England and 2 in Scotland, with an annual intake of about 250 students.

The first special school for children with speech and language disorders was opened at Moor House, Oxted, Surrey, in 1947; the second, the John Horniman School, at Worthing, Sussex, in 1958; and a third special school will shortly be opened in Nottingham.

By 1972, about 930 speech therapists were employed whole- or part-time (in total they were equivalent to 600 whole-time therapists) in 1,600 school health service clinics, where they treated about 104,000 school children. There continues to be an acute shortage of speech therapists, especially in the predominantly industrial areas.

Most of the children who attend speech therapy clinics have slight defects of articulation that do not affect their language development; and most of them acquire normal articulation by the age of 7 or 8 years. A survey of over 2,000 children aged 5 years in all the primary schools of Leicester in 1964, by a medical officer of the Department of Education and Science in association with the Authority's speech therapists, found that 85 per cent of the children had normal speech; 12 per cent had a 'possible slight defect of speech mainly affecting single consonants'; and 3 per cent had defects requiring further investigation (Department of Education and Science, 1966a).

In the early 1950s a few speech therapists proposed the employment of unqualified assistants to relieve them of the more routine work with children with slight articulation defects and so enable them to give more time to the minority of children who stammered, had cleft palate, or had language disorders. The proposal was not generally welcomed but, even so, one or two assistants were appointed. About 20 years later the Quirk Committee concluded that the 'use of an aide might save perhaps a third of a speech therapist's time' (Department of Education and Science, 1972f).

In the early years of the school health service the treatment of stammerers was about the beginning and end of speech therapy for school children. There have been almost as many methods of treating stammerers as there were speech therapists; the cause of the condition and the results of treatment are still controversial.

The most notable development in speech therapy services has been the increasing attention given to children with language disorders and to those whose defective speech is due to neurological or other anatomical impairment. These children, although only a small minority of those with defective speech, present difficult problems of diagnosis, education, and treatment. Much still has to be learnt about them; and they require the services not only of speech therapists but also of various medical specialists, psychologists, audiologists, and teachers. With language impaired children it is difficult to distinguish between education and treatment; often the teacher is as much therapist as the therapist is teacher. What is certain is that school children with disorders of language require a school, not hospital, centred diagnostic and treatment service if they are to derive most benefit from their education and treatment.

Educationally Subnormal Children

Following the Education Act of 1870 special classes for feeble-minded children were started in some elementary schools by a few local education authorities. The Elementary Education (Defective and Epileptic Children) Act of 1899 encouraged more education authorities to provide for these children. When the school health service was established in 1908 educational provision for feeble-minded children was considered to be 'wholly inadequate'. This was thought to have been due, in part at least, to the expense involved (at that time it cost from £10 to £12 a year to educate mentally and physically handicapped children in day schools, and from £25 to £35 in residential schools) and to the 'degree of doubt' in the minds of many educationalists 'as to the wisdom of expending

19

large sums of money in educating children whose future usefulness seems so gravely limited as in the case of the feeble-minded.' In consequence, the Board of Education recommended that school doctors should inquire into the mental as well as the physical condition of the children (Board of Education, 1910*f*). In 1909 the Board issued a Schedule of Medical Examination of Children for Mental Defect to assist school doctors in their examination of children suspected of mental defect (Board of Education, 1910*f*).

The Mental Deficiency Act of 1913 classified the mentally handicapped as idiots, imbeciles, and feeble-minded; responsibility for the education and training of the feeble-minded remained with the education authorities, and of the idiots and imbeciles with the health authorities. In 1914 education authorities were given the duty to provide special classes for children certified as feeble-minded, admission being restricted to those who had been certified. The Education Act of 1944 substituted the term 'educational subnormality' for mental defective, abolished certification, and prescribed a procedure (that distressed many parents) for ascertaining children considered to be unsuitable for education at school and who were the responsibility of the local health or hospital authorities. The Education (Handicapped Children) Act of 1970, which came into force in April, 1971, abolished this procedure and transferred responsibility for the education and training of all mentally handicapped children from the health to the education authorities.

Thus, it took 100 years from the passing of the Education Act of 1870 to bring all mentally handicapped children into the general educational system. When the 1970 Act came into force there were about 24,000 children in over 300 training centres, including over 3,000 in special care units, 8,000 in about 100 hospitals, and an uncertain number at home or in private institutions. All these children are now regarded as educationally subnormal and about 400 special schools have been formed from the provision existing at the time of transfer of responsibility.

Although many pathological conditions are known to give rise to mental handicap—known causes being more common among the most severely handicapped—the cause is not known in most affected children. A survey of over 500 children during 1965–1969, in the West Riding of Yorkshire, who were considered to be unsuitable for education at school on account of severe mental handicap, found that about 80 per cent of them had, or probably had, pathological conditions that had affected their mental development; only a few of them had suffered post-natal brain damage (Smith, 1971). Further research may reveal more causes of this common condition.

Developmental screening tests of function and screening tests for biochemical disturbances, that are being used increasingly in the periodic examination of pre-school children, are helping to identify more mentally handicapped children at an earlier age than in former years.

The preliminary assessment of mental handicap in young children may, in future, be made more frequently in health centres and paediatric out-patient departments of hospitals by multi-disciplinary teams. But, assessment to be worth the name will have to continue in an educational setting if the learning difficulties of the children are to be properly studied and assessed.

In 1964 the Ministry of Education restated its views on what constituted educational subnormality: 'Educational backwardness is not regarded as a single, sharply defined characteristic as was mental deficiency but rather as a matter of degree and origin, and caused by a combination of circumstances. . . . nor is special education looked upon as a form of education peculiar to special schools' (Ministry of Education, 1964). The educational category 'educationally subnormal' now comprises children who are mentally handicapped as well as those who are educationally retarded as a result of other conditions such as poor health, physical or emotional disorders, irregular school attendance, poor teaching, unsatisfactory home circumstances, and conditions that are now loosely described as specific learning difficulties (such as specific developmental dyslexia).

Many children in the other educational categories of handicap are also educationally subnormal. In recent years the school health and school psychological services have co-operated closely, and with the teachers, in the ascertainment and assessment of all these children. It is essential that they continue to do so.

The ascertainment and assessment of educationally subnormal children have always been important duties of school doctors: duties that they have carried out conscientiously and skilfully and for which they took additional training.[3] The development of special educational services for these boys and girls owes much to them.

Delicate and Physically Handicapped Children

In 1899 the first day school for crippled children to be recognised by the Board of Education was opened at the Passmore Edwards Settlement in London. The Residential School for Convalescent Children at West Kirby, Cheshire, was recognised in 1902. In 1905 the Manchester Education Authority established the first local education authority school for physically defective children, at Swinton House, Pendlebury. In 1907 the first open air school in this country was opened by the London County Council at Bostall Wood, Plumstead.

The schools for crippled children (re-named physically handicapped by the Handicapped Pupils and School Health Service Regulations, 1945) were established primarily for children with tuberculosis of bones and joints, heart disease, congenital physical defects, rickets, severe anaemia, and malnutrition. Schools were also provided in a few hospitals for the treatment of surgical diseases in children.

Open air schools were for children who were debilitated, undernourished, subject to frequent attacks of bronchial catarrh or 'incipient pulmonary tuberculosis', or who were 'nervous and excitable', and who were unable to attend ordinary schools with moderate regularity. Some of these schools were specifically for tuberculous children who were considered not to require hospital treatment

---

[3] The first course of post-graduate training was held in 1921 by the National Association for the Care of the Mentally Handicapped, that later merged with the National Association for Mental Health when the courses became the joint responsibility of the N.A.M.H. and the University of London. At first, the courses were of one week's duration but were extended, by stages, to four weeks. They were terminated in 1973, by which time other courses had been provided by several university departments and institutes of child health. During these 50 years about 4,000 school and other doctors attended N.A.M.H. courses.

but who were unable to benefit from instruction in ordinary schools; in course of time, however, this separate form of provision ceased. In some areas open air classes for debilitated, undernourished children were held in the playgrounds of elementary schools, or in public parks or other open spaces. Some of the first schools to be established, notably those in London, were open from 9 am to 7 pm.

By 1931, there were 80 day open air schools for 9,000 children and 45 residential schools for 3,000 children; 8 day schools for 600 children and 37 residential schools for 1,700 children with pulmonary tuberculosis; 59 day schools for 6,000 children and 25 residential schools for 1,250 children who were cripples; and 45 hospital schools for 4,500 children (Board of Education, 1931b).

Delicate Children

The special features of the early open air schools were: smaller classes and shorter hours than in ordinary schools; they remained open during ordinary school holidays; a midday rest period for all the children; school meals (often 3 meals a day); 'as much fresh air and sunshine as possible'; and regular medical and nursing supervision (Board of Education, 1910d).

These schools were of great benefit to many children, and were a boon to the school health service confronted by large numbers of debilitated children from poor homes and a paucity of general medical services for them. Indeed, the expansion of open air schools was due largely to the advocacy and efforts of school doctors and nurses; all through the years there has been a strong working partnership between the school health service and the schools for delicate and physically handicapped children.

In consequence of the big improvement in the health and physique of school children, and in economic and social conditions generally, in the 40 years following the establishment of the school health service, a survey of all the open air schools in England and Wales, by four medical officers of the Ministry of Education, was made in 1949–1950. The survey covered 10,500 children in 127 schools. The total school population was about 5½ million. Respiratory diseases (chiefly asthma, bronchitis and bronchiectasis) and debility from illness or unsatisfactory home circumstances were the main conditions accounting for the admission of children to these schools; an increasing number of 'nervous' children, and of maladjusted children, were also being admitted; in some of the schools many children were contacts of relatives with tuberculosis.

The conclusion of the doctors making the survey was that there was still a need for special schools for delicate children, especially for those in the more industrial areas, but that there was no justification for much expansion of existing provision. They recommended also that the spartan open air conditions that some of the schools continued to provide should cease (Ministry of Education, 1952).

By 1971, when the school population had increased to over 8 million, the number of delicate children in special schools had fallen to just under 7,000; in addition, about 900 were being educated in independent schools, in hospitals, in special classes apart from special schools, or at home (Department of Education and Science, 1972g). Asthma, bronchitis, debility, and emotional disturbance were the main conditions presented by the children; many of them were severely affected.

22

Physically Handicapped Children

In the early days of the school health service the chief causes of physical handicap in school children were tuberculosis of bones and joints, chronic rheumatic heart disease, paralysis from poliomyelitis, and congenital defects. The first three diseases have virtually been eliminated by advances in medical treatment or by vaccination. Much of the physical defect in children is due now to congenital or hereditary causes: cerebral palsy, spina bifida, congenital heart defect, and congenital deformities of limbs are the main conditions causing physical handicap in childhood. Modern methods of treatment have also saved the lives of many children with congenital defects (for example, spina bifida) who formerly would have died in infancy or early childhood.

This is not always sheer gain. What sort of life are boys and girls likely to have who, as a result of having been born with a severe degree of spina bifida, are confined to a wheel chair; had to have early surgical treatment and have to wear a urinary bag all their lives, on account of incontinence of urine, with continuing serious risk of urinary infection and permanent kidney damage; have to have a tube inserted into their brain to prevent hydrocephalus yet live with the ever-present, grave risk of increasing intracranial pressure, from blockage or non-functioning of the tube and valve in their skull, that may lead to mental retardation or, sometimes, blindness?

What of the children born with severe limb deformities, a few with only a vestige of legs and arms? Or of the children severely affected by cerebral palsy?

For many of them the outlook is bleak. As they grow older they become more aware of the consequences of their infirmity; of their social isolation; of their dependence on others. They become an increasingly heavy burden on their families and many of them will require community care for the whole of their lives. Is there any wonder that the question is being asked: Why strive with all the aids and resources of modern medicine to preserve these children's lives at all costs? This is a highly emotive question involving profound ethical considerations. But, it is a question that is being asked by an increasing number of parents who carry a grievous burden that sometimes affects their health, and may have deleterious effects on the rest of the family. The anxiety that this problem creates in parents often persists all through their children's school years, and has to be taken into account by teachers as well as by the school health service. It is a problem that seldom confronted their predecessors.

There is evidence, however, that since about 1972–1973 fewer babies with a severe degree of spina bifida are being subjected to surgery. If this trend continues there is likely to be a substantial reduction in the number of children with severe spina bifida surviving beyond infancy, and a consequential reduction in the number of special school places required.

Most children with severe physical handicap have learning difficulties of one kind or another; and many have more than one disability. They all require assessment, treatment, and supervision from infancy through their school years. They demand much attention from the school health service which, increasingly, works in collaboration with the teachers, the school psychological service, and the hospitals the children periodically attend.

23

Although the school health service during its early years was almost wholly concerned with the physical health of children, and with those who were then considered to be mentally defective, some consideration was also given to boys and girls who were 'nervous and excitable'. In his first Annual Report the Chief Medical Officer of the Board of Education, in 1908, expressed the opinion that 'nervous' children were likely to benefit from attendance at open air schools (Board of Education, 1910*e*).

Interest in 'nervous' children slowly developed. 'Neuropathic' children were first mentioned by the Chief Medical Officer in his Report for 1920 when he described their behaviour as being 'marked by certain psychological characteristics, a tendency to quarrel, to make violent friendships, to engender bitter dislikes, to attend unduly to his bodily functions, to night terrors, to unreasonable fears, grief, abnormal introspection and self examination, and to separation from family and friends. The physical accompaniment of these psychical symptoms may include loss of sleep, constipation, diarrhoea, sickness, stammering, fainting, resentment of change of diet and scene, for no assignable reason.' Despite all this, it was considered that some of these children might 'eventually rise to a high career in public affairs' (Board of Education, 1921*a*).

The Report for 1920 also gave the results of a survey of children attending a 'slum school' in Notting Hill, London, in 1912–1920, when it was found that 12 per cent of the children in 1912–13, 26·5 per cent in 1915–16, 31·6 per cent in 1917–18, and 18·1 per cent in 1919–20 had 'neuropathic conditions.'

The terms 'maladjusted' and 'child guidance' first appeared in the Annual Reports of the Chief Medical Officer of the Board of Education in the Report for 1927 when he mentioned that increasing interest was being taken by school medical officers and educationalists generally in 'nervous', 'unstable', 'maladjusted' and 'difficult' children (Board of Education, 1928*b*). Among the school doctors taking a particular interest in these children were those of Birmingham, London, and Stoke-on-Trent. As early as 1913 the London County Council was the first local education authority to appoint an educational psychologist.

It was in 1927 that the Jewish Health Organization established the East London Child Guidance Clinic, the first to be set up in this country. The first to be opened by a local education authority was in Birmingham, in 1932; that year, also, the first local education authority special school for maladjusted children was opened in Leicester. By 1939 only 22 child guidance clinics had been provided by local education authorities.

The mass evacuation of school children from congested urban areas in the early days of the Second World War quickly brought to light large numbers of boys and girls who were considered to be 'unbilletable' on account of their antisocial behaviour; soon there were widespread demands for psychiatric and psychological services for them. When the War ended the number of child guidance clinics had increased to 79.

In 1950, the Minister of Education appointed a Committee to inquire into the medical, educational, and social problems of maladjusted children with reference to their treatment within the educational system. The Committee reported in 1955 (Ministry of Education, 1955). This Report greatly stimulated the development of services for children with behaviour difficulties. By 1970, over 400 child guidance clinics had been provided by local education authorities that were attended by 70,000 children; and over 11,000 maladjusted boys and girls were attending special or independent schools, or special classes in ordinary schools. The percentage of the school population attending child guidance clinics varied greatly from area to area: in 1967, for example, on average, one pupil in 124 in England and Wales attended these clinics; the rates ranged from one in 87 in Southern England to one in 238 in Northern England; it was one in 108 in Newcastle upon Tyne and one in 1976 in Northumberland; one in 54 in Liverpool and one in 1,078 in Birkenhead. There were similar variations in the percentages of children considered to require education in special schools or classes on account of maladjustment; in 1970 the national average was 16·5 per 10,000 school population, but the rates ranged from 6 per 10,000 in the North of England to 23 per 10,000 in South-East England, and to 37 per 10,000 in Greater London (Department of Education and Science, 1969). Although several factors could be cited partly to explain these variations there can be no doubt that different standards of assessment were adopted in different areas.

An increasing number of school doctors and hospital paediatricians are themselves dealing with children with behaviour and emotional problems, and advising their parents, while referring specially difficult cases to psychiatrists.

Autistic Children. In recent years attention has been attracted to a group of emotionally disturbed and retarded children who seem unable to make human relationships, are disinterested in their surroundings, and appear to live in a world of their own. Their language and speech development is delayed and disordered; and they have outbursts of disruptive behaviour. They were termed autistic in 1943 (Kanner, 1943).

It has been estimated that there are about 4 autistic children per 10,000 school population—about 4,000 in England and Wales (Wing, O'Connor, and Lotter, 1967). Suggestions on educational provision for autistic children were published by the Department of Education and Science in 1971 (Department of Education and Science, 1971a).

Drug Taking. The number of older school children and young persons who experiment with drugs is not known. The majority of those who do take drugs do so for the fun of it, as a manifestation of their approaching adulthood, and with no intention of becoming dependent on drugs. A minority are emotionally disturbed or come from unsatisfactory homes—but not by any means always financially poor homes; these children and young people are at increased risk of progressing from 'soft' to 'hard' drugs, of associating with drug addicts, and of becoming delinquent.

There are, as yet, no specific signs and symptoms that can lead to the early detection of boys and girls who take drugs; uncharacteristic behaviour is often the first sign but this may also be due to a variety of causes. Drug taking by school children is a relatively recent development; although serious it has to be kept in perspective. This is yet another problem that can best be handled by the teachers in close collaboration with the school health service and the parents. The Department of Education and Science published a pamphlet on the subject in 1972 (Department of Education and Science, 1972*h*).

The dangers to health from smoking tobacco (that is a major factor in the development of coronary heart disease, chronic bronchitis, and in the 30,000 deaths annually in England and Wales from lung cancer), and from alcoholism (a minimum estimate is that there are 300,000 alcoholics in England and Wales), have been of growing concern to the school health service and teachers since cigarette smoking is often started in later childhood and early youth, and since more young people are now taking alcohol in one form or another. More prominence is being given to these subjects in health education in schools. No doubt the health education that is given in schools could be improved, more perhaps in some schools than in others, but this is not an easy or short-term subject. It is one that has to be dealt with, and seen by the children to be dealt with, with conviction. The influence of home life is greater than that of even the best schools, and both are affected by the attitudes of society at large.

Socially Deprived Children

Although most school children are healthy and have good homes a substantial minority still have a poor start in life that affects their development and their educational and social progress. The total number of children living in divided or broken homes, in poverty, or in slum or near-slum conditions, is not known but it is large.

Over 81,000 children under 16 years of age in England and Wales had parents who were divorced in 1971; many of these parents married when they were under 20 years of age. In 1971, also, 65,000 children were born illegitimate (Registrar General, 1973*a*)—and these are figures for one year only.

In 1970, about 80,000 children were in the care of local authorities (Home Office, 1970*a*).

In recent years there has been a large increase in the number of children, aged 10–16 years, found guilty of indictable offences, mainly theft of one form or another: in 1968 about 57,000 boys and 7,000 girls were convicted (Home Office, 1970*b*).

A study of 13 year old boys in approved schools in England and Wales in 1962 found that a third of them came from broken homes and 13 per cent were illegitimate (Field, Hammond, and Tizard, 1970).

In 1972, supplementary benefits were paid to 433,000 families with children, 32,000 families having five or more dependent children. Family income supplement was paid in respect of 188,000 children (Department of Health and Social Security, 1973*c*).

In October, 1972, over 850,000 school children (just over one in 10) were receiving free school meals.

It was, therefore, hardly surprising that a study of slow learners in secondary schools in 1967–68 found that adverse social conditions were 'widespread' among these educationally retarded boys and girls (Department of Education and Science, 1971*b*).

26

The school health service has always been concerned with the welfare of socially deprived children. It is depressing that despite the greatly improved economic and social circumstances of the population generally there are still hundreds of thousands of families living in poor economic and social conditions. Although the education and school health services can help these unfortunate children, perhaps even more so than they have done in past years, the real remedy lies elsewhere.

Assessment of Handicapped Children

The assessment of handicapped children has been an inescapable duty of the school health service ever since it started. How could children have been ascertained as requiring, or continuing to require, special education if their degree of handicap, their capabilities and potentialities, and their response to education were not 'assessed'? Indeed, in the early years of the school health service handicapped children had to be 'certified' by school doctors before they could be admitted to special schools. Nowadays, there are some who appear to think that an assessment centre is a new concept, and that the establishment of such centres in regional and district hospitals is a revolutionary advance; they either do not know, or have failed to grasp, the extent of the 'assessment' of handicapped children carried out over the years by school doctors, ear, nose and throat surgeons, ophthalmologists, orthopaedic surgeons, and psychiatrists employed through the school health service in school clinics and special schools, with the help of teachers and the school psychological service. Admittedly, not all areas or all schools were equally well served; and with increasing knowledge other professional workers (such as audiologists, neurologists, and speech therapists) became, or ought to have become, involved, particularly in the investigation and 'assessment' of children with speech and language disorders.

For many years some special schools have had periodic visits from medical consultants to enable them to observe the children in an educational setting, both at work and at play, and to discuss their progress and difficulties with the teachers and school health service staff.

In 1955, the Committee on Maladjusted Children recommended (Ministry of Education, 1955b) that arrangements should be made for all hostels and schools for maladjusted children 'to be visited regularly by a psychiatrist and to keep in close touch with a child guidance clinic.'

In 1972, the Committee of Enquiry into the Education of the Visually Handicapped recommended (Department of Education and Science, 1972i) that 'all schools for the visually handicapped should be visited regularly by a consultant ophthalmologist and an optician working for the National Health Service on a sessional basis, and should be equipped with a suitable examination room. There should be close co-operation between the ophthalmologist and the teaching staff, and between the optician and the ophthalmologist in the supply and maintenance of spectacles and low visual aids.' The Committee emphasized that it was 'highly desirable' that ophthalmologists should 'observe children at work and discuss them with the staff.'

Similar recommendations involving other consultants could be made with equal force for the other types of special school.

27

The diagnosis and early assessment of the capabilities of children with disabilities, particularly those with physical or mental disabilities, and those with language and speech disorders including the pre-lingually deaf, are often made long before they start school; and this is likely to become the general practice.

Assessment, to be worth the name, must take account not only of a child's disabilities (and many children have more than one) but of his development, of his reaction to learning and life at school, and, of increasing importance, of his aptitudes and fitness for employment. Thus, although the assessment of handicapped children may first be made in hospitals, to be fully effective it must continue in the setting of the schools attended, with full account taken of their educational difficulties and progress, or lack of progress, and with the teachers and educational psychologists as essential members of the assessment team. Full account must be taken also of the children's home circumstances and of parental attitudes throughout the years of the children's school life; and towards the end of school life of the views and advice of the youth employment service.

If the best interests of the children are to continue to be served educational and medical assessment must not be separated in the way that educational and medical services are separately organised. It would be disastrous for the children if medical assessment were to become a matter for hospital paediatric clinics and educational assessment for the schools, with transmission of reports between them as their only real link.

Although essential, 'assessment' can be overdone and be overrated by the professionals involved in it, 'Assessment' is not an end in itself; it is as much in need of continuing evaluation (another fashionable process at risk of over usage) as any other service; but, who will evaluate the evaluers?

The primary requirements for handicapped children are skilled, individual teaching and training, and, when their school days are over, employment, sheltered or otherwise, for those of them who are fit for work. Medically, the greatest need is for research into the causes of handicapping disabilities with a view to their prevention. Retrolental fibroplasia from too high a concentration of oxygen at birth; congenital limb and other deformities from thalidomide taken by mothers in the early weeks of pregnancy; blindness, deafness, heart deformity, and mental retardation from rubella, an apparently mild communicable disease, are—although they were disastrous for many children—promising indicators that the causes of other handicapping deformities may yet be found and then prevented.

Changing Pattern of Disability in School Children

During the period 1913–1915, on average, 11 per cent of school leavers when examined at school were found to be malnourished; 4 to 6 per cent had heart disease; 67–72 per cent had dental caries; 5 per cent had unclean bodies; and in some schools from 30 to 60 per cent of the girls had verminous heads (Board of Education, 1918). Communicable diseases were rife, especially diphtheria and tuberculosis, and rheumatic fever killed or disabled thousands of children.

In 1907 over 3,000 children aged 5–14 years died from tuberculosis; 4 died in 1971. From 1938 to 1971 deaths of children aged 5–14 years from diphtheria

28

fell from almost 3,000 to one; from rheumatic fever and chronic rheumatic heart disease from 914 to 7; from pneumonia from 634 to 140; from diseases of the ear and mastoid from 230 to 8; from osteomyelitis from 150 to one; from epilepsy from 129 to 34; and from diabetes from 69 to 16. As recently as 1947, 2,700 children aged 5–14 years contracted poliomyelitis of whom 168 died. Inactivated poliomyelitis vaccine was introduced in 1957, and live oral vaccine in 1962. In 1971, only 3 children developed the disease of whom 2 died (Registrar General 1973*b*).

Tuberculosis, rheumatic fever, and poliomyelitis not only killed many children but left many of the survivors severely crippled. In 1912, about 900 children severely disabled by tuberculosis of bones and joints were in the London special schools; by 1964 there were only 31 in all the special schools in England and Wales. In 1928, 1,250 children with rheumatic heart disease were in the London special schools for physically handicapped children; by 1964 there were only 76 in all these schools throughout the country (Department of Education and Science 1966*b*). As recently as 1964 about 600 children crippled by poliomyelitis were in the special schools for the physically handicapped; by 1970 the number had fallen to 316 (Department of Education and Science, 1972*b*). If vaccination against poliomyelitis is maintained this disease will virtually disappear.

These dramatic improvements in child mortality and morbidity have resulted from immunization and vaccination, modern drug therapy, and better economic and environmental conditions.

The expectation of life at birth for a boy was 48 years in 1901–1910, and 69 years in 1971; for a girl it was 52 years in 1901–1910 and 75 years in 1971 (Registrar General 1973*a*).

The chief causes of death of children aged 5–14 years (in descending order of frequency) in 1971 were: accidents (1,024 deaths), cancer including leukaemia (523 deaths), congenital malformations (282 deaths), and respiratory diseases (225 deaths). In those aged 15–19 years accidents accounted for 1,318, cancer for 225, respiratory diseases for 145, and congenital malformations for 78 (Registrar General 1973*b*).

The prevalence of respiratory diseases can be further reduced; there is evidence (Colley, Douglas, and Reid, 1973) that air pollution and adverse social class conditions have an important part in the development of respiratory diseases in early childhood, and that those with such a history are more liable to respiratory disease in adult life, particularly so if they are cigarette smokers. Asthma still presents a baffling problem; surveys of school children (Smith, 1961; and Rutter, Tizard, and Whitmore, 1970) suggest that about 150,000 children are affected; as mentioned earlier many asthmatic children attend special schools for delicate children for a period, and school doctors hold special sessions for asthmatic children in over 60 school clinics.

Congenital disabilities account for much of the handicap in school children, particularly blindness, pre-lingual deafness, other physical handicaps such as cerebral palsy, spina bifida, and heart defect, and mental handicap. Genetically determined diseases such as cystic fibrosis, haemophilia, and muscular dystrophy are also important causes of handicap. All these conditions affect the children's education and development and are of continuing concern to the school health service.

Over the years the prevalence of skin diseases such as impetigo, ringworm, and scabies has fluctuated but many fewer children are now affected.

Although it is now rare to find body lice or fleas among children at school, and most of them are clean, it is disappointing that about a quarter of a million were found with nits or lice in their hair in 1970 (Department of Education and Science, 1972*j*). Admittedly, the percentage was 10 or more times greater when the school health service started but, even so, there is no cause for satisfaction in the present lower incidence: all children should be clean and without vermin. Many of those infested come from socially deprived homes and areas and this is another indication of the plight of children in these districts.

The nutrition of children has greatly improved. Better economic conditions leading to a higher standard of living for more people; school meals; the teaching of food values, cookery, and household management in schools, have all contributed to improved nutrition. Indeed, some children are now malnourished from excess of food, especially carbohydrate foods, and are overweight for their age.

Not only are school children of better physique than their predecessors when the school health service started but they reach physical maturity earlier: on average, girls attain puberty at about the age of 13 years, and boys at about 15 years. All have to remain at school until they are 16 years old, and an increasing number remain until they are 17 or 18 years of age. The school health service and the schools are dealing not only with boys and girls but also with young men and women.

School doctors and nurses have become involved increasingly in health education in schools. Sixty years ago the teaching of hygiene in elementary schools was considered to be 'an integral part of the ordinary school routine, . . . a practice rather than a theory, a way of life rather than an abstract idea' (Board of Education, 1914*b*); but, in practice, health education comprised little more than the teaching of simple hygiene and the instruction of girls in very elementary child care and mothercraft. Now, health education is 'concerned with a vast and varied field touching many branches of science . . .; it involves every type of school, children of all kinds, parents, teachers, all of us. And its claim must be pursued not in the abstract realm of academic theory, but in the demanding context of a good general education that will meet the needs of our time' (Department of Education and Science, 1968*b*).

There is still much criticism that young people leave school with a very inadequate understanding of the working of their own bodies, of personal relationships, and of such subjects of social importance as illegitimacy, premarital conception, birth control and abortion; and that many of them are ill-prepared for the responsibilities of early marriage that so many of them undertake. Ignorance of these vital human and social problems is not confined to duller pupils; some university and college students have been described as being in 'appalling ignorance of sexual matters' (Binnie, 1971). Of course, some schools do more than others but there is no doubt that schools, and school doctors and nurses, could, and should, do much more to make health education in schools, particularly for older pupils, appear more relevant to the circumstances of the times.

Although the school health service has long been concerned with children from poverty-stricken homes, with the physically handicapped, and with those with emotional and behaviour problems, it has become increasingly so in the past 20 to 30 years when diseases that once ravaged childhood have been brought under control or have been virtually eliminated. It always has been mainly a preventive rather than a curative health service. All through the years it has been alive to the educational aspects of its work: to the effects that disabilities and personal difficulties of all kinds have on the education and development of children and young people. It has been concerned more with individual children than with the group. And early on it learnt the need for full co-operation with other professional workers, non-medical as well as medical, and not least with teachers, psychologists, and administrators. This was not always easy; some, inevitably, and in all professions, are better team members than others.

The changing pattern of disability in childhood has, probably, affected hospital paediatricians even more than the school health service. This subject was the theme of the inaugural lecture of the present Professor of Child Health at the University of Dundee (Mitchell, 1973) who said that 'The academic subject of child health has developed considerably in the past quarter of a century, however, and its content has been transformed in response to the altered pattern of paediatric practice. It is likely to change further in the next few years, as the medical profession becomes increasingly aware of its responsibilities in the wider issues which affect child life and health. . . . As major diseases become fewer in number and variety, and are more effectively dealt with, the doctor will be increasingly involved with social and preventive aspects of medicine.'

That is precisely what school doctors have been involved in right from the start of the service. The school health service has been intimately concerned with the educational aspects of disability, whether mental, physical, or social. It is crucial that the *educational* aspect of 'paediatric practice' retains, and, indeed, increases its emphasis when the school health service becomes part of the National Health Service.

Thirty or more years ago school doctors realized that their previous professional training had not equipped them properly to deal with the changing pattern of disability in children and young people. Shortly after the Second World War the Society of Medical Officers of Health (notably its School Health and Maternity and Child Health Groups) organised short refresher courses on a variety of subjects. The courses varied in length and content and ultimately included one of six weeks duration on developmental paediatrics. These courses had a strong educational content and non-medical lecturers had a large part in them; they pointed the need, and, indeed, the direction for longer courses organized by university departments of child health in association with university institutes or departments of education and other specialist departments.

In short, there will be no child health service worth the name in this country unless the school health and hospital paediatric services work together in full and equal partnership, and with the teachers and the school psychological service *in* the schools and colleges, and with the parents and the family doctors.

'The Health of the School Child'

This issue of 'The Health of the School Child' is the last in a series of reports that started in 1910. The first report, termed the Annual Report of the Chief Medical Officer of the Board of Education, was for the year 1908.

The report for 1912–13 gave the cost of the school medical service as just over £$\frac{1}{2}$ million; in 1969–70 it was over £24 million.

The Chief Medical Officer wrote in his report for 1920 that although the service had to deal with the mass of elementary school children, 'each defective or ailing child must be handled as an individual' (Board of Education 1921b). And it was in 1921 that the report was given the title 'The Health of the School Child.'

The report for 1939 was the last one to be published annually; a single issue covered the War Years 1939–45; thereafter the report was published biennially, except for the years 1966–68 which were covered by one report published in 1969.

From the start this series of reports has been concerned with the physical and mental health of school children, and with the effects of debility and disability on children's development and education. Inevitably, the earlier reports were concerned mainly with the physical condition of children; but, in recent years, with better physical health and improved economic and social conditions increasing attention was given to children's behaviour and emotional problems, to personal relationships in the setting of health education, to their language and speech disorders, to their physical disabilities, and to their social circumstances.

All through the years these reports were concerned to show that the professional staff of the central and local government departments were colleagues in every sense of the word, the one dependent on the other; and that the school health service was a school, a child, and a parent-orientated service.

The reports also tried to high-light new developments in the health care and supervision of school children by local education authorities and their school health service staffs, as well as publicising special investigations by individual members of the service. The reports were, perhaps, read as much by educationists as by health workers; that was certainly one of the aims of those who contributed to them.

The earlier reports were much concerned with the administration and organisation of the service, and with the relationship which should be established between it and the public health service. Now, the concern is about the organisation of the school health service within the National Health Service and its relationship with the hospital paediatric and general medical practitioner branches of the National Health Service, and, not least, with the Education Service which must be close and continuing.

It would appear that, although there will no longer be 'The Health of the School Child' to comment on these relationships, particularly between the school health and education services, there will be as much need in the future for a periodic and comprehensive review of the work of the school health service as there ever was in the past.

School Dental Service

The first school dental clinic was established at Cambridge in 1907 by means of a gift from a private benefactor. The first report of the Chief Medical Officer of the Board of Education in 1908 describes the premises as being 'two small rooms in a garden, one used as a waiting room supplied with toys for the diversion of the children and the other being the surgery suitably fitted.' It was from these small beginnings that the present service developed. After the passing of the Education (Administrative Provisions) Act the local authority decided to take over the Cambridge Institute as an educational concern and the first whole time school dentist, Mr. E. W. Gant, was appointed in March 1909. Mr. Gant had already acted as a dentist to the Institution replacing Mr. A. T. Simpson who was employed for a brief period in 1907. The estimated total annual expenditure for the Cambridge clinic was £410 which included the dentist's salary, £300, and that of his chairside assistant £39.

The Board of Education had sanctioned arrangements for dental services in 55 local education authorities by 1909. There was a lack of uniformity in dental reports and this perturbed the Board and the condition of children's teeth was alarming. Nor was there a significant amount of conservative work available to children and several hundred had to be examined before the dentist discovered a tooth that had been filled. John Knowles, the school dentist at Bradford, examined 8,657 children in 1910 and found only six fillings.

In the 1911 report from Shropshire's Medical Officer only 7% of five year old children and 4% of twelve year olds were found to have sound teeth and one must consider these findings against a background of little or no treatment. The need for a dental service was unquestionable and the Board consistently promoted its growth. The pioneers in the field painstakingly noted the conditions they had found and carried out the simple surveys of that period supplemented by questionnaires which are still of interest. In Shropshire in 1911 a sweet consumption classification was adopted for the then current caries research. The questionnaire listed four categories under which it was expected the majority of children could be numbered in relation to their sweet eating habits.

1. Large number of sweets eaten—almost every day.
2. Considerable quantities eaten—several times a week.
3. Few sweets eaten—almost once a week.
4. No sweets at all eaten.

The results of the survey were described as striking and sweets were named as one of the potent causes of dental caries.

The writers were aware of the deficiencies of the survey and point to the vagueness of the classification but their claim was that in the aggregate the classifications were sufficiently correct. Surveys on the use of the tooth brush were also being carried out and its usefulness and its limitations were being noted. In a survey in 13 schools in the East End, using suitable controls, the researchers concluded that 'so far as concerns the prevention or arrest of dental decay the usefulness of the tooth brush particularly as ordinarily employed is strictly limited'.

It would seem that children were not any more difficult to treat in the early days if they were approached in a manner deemed to be reasonable and given

33

regular treatment. Mr. W. H. Jones in his report from Cambridge in 1912 states 'with the 27 exceptions mentioned as 'intractable' the remaining 4,208 children were admirable. They evinced intelligent interest in the work. The tradition of tooth treatment has now become fixed in their minds as part of school life. It has no terrors, perhaps because no deception is ever attempted and the success of the scheme rests on its simplicity and the resulting confidence of the children'. Mr. Jones had a keen sense of observation and noted in 1912 that dental disease was contagious: his opinion was stated boldly and he was convinced that a good treatment service would lessen the amount of oral sepsis in the home. 'In consequence the younger children breathe a better atmosphere in—eat and drink from vessels less liable to be contaminated'. The Board accorded Mr. Jones a bouquet for his observations and the accuracy of his statistics but there will be few dentists today who would not be impressed by his reasoning. His statements passed into oblivion and it was half a century later that the premise of infective dental caries was receiving attention.

It was necessary to proclaim the aims and to set desirable standards for the school dental service. In 1912 the Board devoted a chapter in its report to 'the Basis of a Satisfactory Dental Scheme'. The scheme is more impressive in retrospect for its good advice rather than for any deficiencies exposed by time. After specifying that the critical age for treatment is the time of the emergence of the permanent teeth it makes the following point: 'The treatment should be conservative in character and accordingly the bulk of the treatment work should be by filling rather than by extraction. Conservative dentistry includes also preventive measures such as extraction work as contributes to the preservation of the dentition as a whole and any mechanical devices necessary to regulate the teeth.' The scheme has been revised at intervals between 1912 to 1962 but there is little doubt that the publication of such schemes have played an important part in ensuring the necessary standards in children's dentistry.

The school dentist of 60 years ago was aware of the need for dental health education and in Sheffield addresses had been given at Mothers' Meetings and lantern lectures soon followed to teachers and to training college students, women inspectors and school nurses. If the hopes of these dentists were higher than the results achieved this is understandable for they were motivated by idealism and were convinced that if the public were only educated then habits would inevitably change. 'This is true prevention' states the Kettering report of 1913 and 'there is I think reasonable grounds for the hope that by this means alone a great deal will in the future be done to check the ravages of dental disease'.

In 1914 the first mobile dental clinic was in use in Norfolk. 'This is a lightly constructed four-wheeled van about 9 ft × 6 in, by 6 ft 0 in inside, fitted with proper chair for dentistry together with suitable cupboards, lavatory and stove. It is well lighted and ventilated and fitted with folding doors and steps approached from the back and with covered seat in front for the driver'. The mobile unit worked well according to a report of the time which gave this sober appraisal 'The value of the work is beyond dispute but the drafting of a scheme to cover a large area presents many difficulties and experience alone can indicate the best way to overcome these difficulties'.

The First World War left the service less affected than might have been expected. The first operative ancillary workers were brought into service and in 1917 the report of the Board gives the matter an airing 'A few authorities, finding themselves in difficulty have proposed to the Board that they should use unqualified dental 'dressers' who with the help of the school nurse would it is suggested be able to deal with a large portion of dental work'. The work to be done by the dental dresser would be under the supervision of a qualified dentist and be as follows:

1. He would assist the dentist by inspecting and charting the children,
2. He would undertake the simpler dressing, fillings, scalings and extractions under the supervision of the school dentist.

A departmental committee on the Dentists Act was appointed by the Privy Council in July 1917 and they left wide latitude to the Board of Education to approve the arrangements in particular cases. In 1921 Section 1(3c) of the Dentists Act, the position of the dental dresser was regularised but the conditions of his employment were so restrictive that this ancillary faded out through time as an unprofitable acquisition.

In 1918, 169 authorities had made dental arrangements. There existed 350 school dental clinics staffed with 270 dentists, most of whom were part-time employees. This was to be an important year for the school dental service for the new Education Act made it a duty of the authority to provide treatment for elementary schoolchildren; previously they had only the power to do so. Although the service was short of staff there was less dental disease. It had fallen quite remarkably from the pre-war years and the low prevalence of decay lasted some time after war had ceased. In London 62% of twelve year old children had sound teeth. The Board of Education however thought that at least 1,000 school dentists were necessary to treat the 3 million schoolchildren which it estimated suffered from dental disease. The Board continued to produce its draft schemes for a satisfactory service and these continually pressed for a uniformly high standard in all authorities administering dental services. It was however impossible to monitor the service offered without help for the Board at that time had no inspecting dentists. As a consequence the Board of Education asked Norman Bennett to help assess the value of the service being offered and to decide on measures which would improve it. He was at that time Chairman of the Representative Board of the British Dental Association and the investigation was carried out in 1919. Ten years later another distinguished Chairman of the Representative Board, A. T. Pitts, carried out a similar task making a detailed inspection of 10 representative local authority dental services. The resulting reports were of inestimable value and recommendations were made on staffing, the conditions of work and the need for appointment of a supervising dental officer. The Board in utilising the services of these distinguished children's dentists recognised that 'of all the routine activities of the school medical service the dental service having regard to its importance is the least fully developed'. Dr. Robert Weaver was appointed to the Board in 1929 and was the first of the dental inspectorate. By 1932, 312 out of the 316 local education authorities had organised a school dental service comprising the equivalent of 550 full-time dentists and about 1,300 dental clinics. In the following year the education authority of Heston and Isleworth appointed a part-time orthodontic consultant who was a member of the staff of the Royal Dental Hospital. About that time too a few local authorities appointed supervising dental officers; and dental attendants were replacing trained nurses. By 1938 the number of school dentists

35

had increased to the equivalent of 780 whole-time and the number of school dental clinics to 1,700. Further progress was interrupted by the Second World War.

The effects of this War on the school dental service were greater than those of the First World War. The evacuation of large numbers of schoolchildren produced problems and the Board issued a circular[1] giving guidance to local education authorities of reception areas on treatment arrangements. School dental officers were called up for service and this had a considerable effect by the end of 1940. A further circular[2] was issued to local education authorities advising them on how to make best use of their depleted dental staff. There was however mercifully a reduction in the prevalence of dental caries.

The Education Act of 1944 not only made dental inspections compulsory for all pupils in maintained schools but also gave local education authorities the duty to provide dental treatment for pupils in maintained secondary schools as well as elementary schools. Regulations made under this Act required all local education authorities to appoint a senior dental officer; the Regulations also prescribed standard school dental record cards. By 1947 the equivalent of 920 full-time school dental officers were employed. In the following year the National Health Service came into force and provided a free dental service for the whole population. The demand from the general public for free dental treatment was so great that in the two years following the establishment of the general dental service the equivalent of over 200 full-time dentists left the school dental service for the general dental service. Within 18 months the school dental service had lost more of its effective strength than had been the case during the whole period of the 1939–1945 War. In 1952 the number of school dentists again began to increase, due mainly to the engagement of part-time dentists who were also working within the general dental service; by the end of 1953 the equivalent of 945 full-time dental officers were employed.

The Education (Miscellaneous Provisions) Act of 1953 made it clear, (there had been some legal doubt about this) that local education authorities had the duty to provide free treatment for children attending their schools. This would be carried out, either by their own dental staff or under arrangements with hospitals in the National Health Service. Regulations made under this act prescribed that senior dental officers were to be designated Principal School Dental Officers. In 1962–63 a Parliamentary Estimates Committee studied the school dental service. A number of criticisms were made and it was suggested that poor local organisation was responsible for low productivity. This led to further appointments to the Departmental Inspectorate and all authorities are visited routinely. There is now the full-time equivalent of 1,437 dentists (1972) working in the local authority dental services in England. In addition there are 218 dental auxiliaries and the recent statistical returns show that they provided treatment for 81,000 pupils, over 51,000 of which were under 9 years of age. Their contribution is of major importance to the dental health of children. There are few dental hygienists within the service and their work is on prophylaxis and dental health education.

---

[1] Circular 1485.
[2] Circular 1523.

Dental Hygienists and Dental Auxiliaries

In 1949 the Ministry of Health arranged with the Eastman Dental Hospital for a one-year training course for dental hygienists. Their main work was to instruct children and adults both individually and in groups in the care of their teeth and to carry out the scaling of teeth and so save their dentists' time for more skilled work. The experimental courses of training at the Eastman Dental Hospital were terminated early in 1954, and in 'The Health of the School Child' for 1952–53 the comment was made 'there appears to be no occasion to qualify the view expressed in 'The Health of the School Child', 1948–49, that hygienists are essentially ancillary workers with a very restricted field of treatment, and that it would be unreasonable to expect their employment to relieve substantially the severe shortage of school dental officers' (Ministry of Education 1954). In 1959 the Manchester Dental School started a course for dental hygienists and some others have since been established. Whilst a more open view would be taken of the dental hygienist at present than in the past very few work within the school service.

On account of the continuing shortage of dentists the Government, in 1950, sent a small team of dentists to New Zealand to study the work of dental nurses who were responsible for much of the treatment given by the New Zealand School Dental Service. The team's report was generally favourable to the employment of dental nurses in the school dental service (United Kingdom Dental Mission 1950).

The Dentists Act 1956 made the dental profession self-governing by providing for the establishment of a General Dental Council with full disciplinary power over dentists. Other provisions were concerned with the training of dental hygienists, and with the introduction of auxiliary dental workers as an experiment on the pattern of the New Zealand system of dental nurses but with a more restricted responsibility for treatment and subject to closer supervision by dentists than in New Zealand. The first training school for dental auxiliaries was opened at New Cross General Hospital, London, in 1960 with a two-year course of training, 218 dental auxiliaries now work in the school dental service and the scheme is no longer experimental.

Fluoridation of Drinking Water Supplies

The Government, in 1952, sent a team to the United States of America to study all aspects of fluoridation in areas where fluoride had been added to drinking water supplies. The team reported (United Kingdom Mission, 1953) that fluoridation of water supplies reduced dental caries in children to a level comparable to that found in areas where fluoride occurs naturally in water, that there was no risk of significant mottling of the teeth if the concentration of added fluoride did not exceed one part per million; and that there was no scientific evidence of any danger to health from this procedure.

The team's recommendations were accepted by the Government and by the medical and dental professions; but by 1973 owing largely to sustained opposition by opponents of fluoridation of water supplies, only about $3\frac{1}{2}$ million of the population of England and Wales lived in areas where fluoride had been added to the drinking water supplies.

Dental Health Education

For many years the school dental service has concerned itself with dental health education. Talks and demonstrations, illustrated by leaflets, posters and films, have been given by school dentists to children and parents. Much advice has been given on diet, and strong efforts made to restrict the sale of biscuits and sweets and to expand the sale of apples and other alternatives to sweets in school tuckshops. Increasingly, dental health has become part of general health education in schools; and the need for early and regular visits to a dentist has been stressed. The expansion of dental services has increased not only the amount of treatment but also opportunities for teaching oral hygiene.

Over the years the quality of dental treatment has much improved. Conservation of teeth is now accepted by most children and parents and this improved pattern is not only due to expansion of the school dental services but also to the introduction of a free general dental service.

The Health Education Council was set up in 1968 and its dental working party now has the task of co-ordinating dental health education but a tribute is due to the Oral Hygiene Service and the General Dental Council both of which played (and continue to play) an important part in the field work.

The Prevalence of Dental Caries in Schoolchildren

Shortly after the outbreak of the second World War school dentists expressed the opinion that the teeth of schoolchildren were less affected than in the pre-war years by dental caries and statistics from Cambridge and studies in London indicated that this was the case. In order to confirm these opinions and to determine the prevalence of dental caries the Ministry set up a dental study in 1948. Several authorities accepted an invitation to arrange for a survey of the teeth of children aged 5 and 12 years. This was the first of a series of quinquennial surveys in 7 areas in England which cover the years 1948–1973 and which at least in the indicative sense is a valid barometer of the prevalence of caries in schoolchildren. The 1948 survey showed that there was less caries in 5 year old children than in pre-war years; reliable information about 12 year old children was not available but it is highly improbable that as many as 19% in the pre-war years showed no signs of caries (Ministry of Education 1949).

The 1953 survey revealed a substantial increase in dental caries; and one carried out in 1958 showed a further increase although it appeared that 'the deterioration of the teeth of children aged 5 had been considerably less between 1953 and 1958 than it was between 1938 and 1953, while the converse is true of the 12 year old group' (Ministry of Education 1960).

It seemed however that the peak in dental disease had been reached for in 1963 there was a substantial decrease in the d.e.f. of 5 year olds and there was a further recorded decrease in both 1968 and 1973. The prevalence of caries in 12 year olds has fallen much less dramatically. Table 1 (a) records the percentage of 5 year old children showing no d.e.f. teeth and indicates a superior position in relation to the dental health of 5 year old children than was the case in 1948. Table 1(b) records a much smaller increase in the percentage of children who are caries free in 12 year old children.

38

TABLE I

(a) 5 Year Olds

Area	Number of Children Examined	Number of Children Showing No d.e.f. teeth	Percentage of Children Showing No d.e.f. Teeth
Manchester	727	192	26·4
Middlesex	1,549	541	34·9
Northumberland ..	5,719	1,644	28·7
Nottinghamshire ..	2,785	785	28·2
Somerset	2,501	629	25·1
West Riding	4,218	963	22·8
East Sussex	989	375	37·9
Total	18,488	5,129	27·8

TABLE I

(b) 12 Year Olds

Area	Number of Children Examined	Number of Children Showing No D.M.F. Teeth	Percentage of Children Showing No D.M.F. Teeth
Manchester	712	54	7·6
Middlesex	1,825	166	9·1
Northumberland ..	5,259	241	4·6
Nottinghamshire ..	2,237	151	6·8
Somerset	2,500	76	3·0
West Riding	4,658	173	3·7
East Sussex	1,650	129	7·8
Total	18,841	990	5·3

Tables 2(a) and 2(b) show the d.e.f. and D.M.F. in 5 year olds and 12 year old children respectively in the 7 authorities involved in the study. Figures 1–4 illustrate the state of dental health of children from 1948 to 1973, whilst figures 5 and 6 give a breakdown of d.e.f. and D.M.F. respectively from 1968–1973 and it is evident that the improvement in small children is not due to an increase in the amount of treatment given to them.

TABLE II

(a) 5 YEAR OLDS

Area	Total Number of d.e.f. Teeth	Total of 'd' Teeth	Total of 'e' Teeth	Total of 'f' Teeth	Average Number of 'd' Teeth per Child	Average Number of 'e' Teeth per Child	Average Number of 'f' Teeth per Child	Total of d.e.f. Teeth
Manchester ..	2,708	1,558	809	341	2·1	1·1	0·5	3·7
Middlesex ..	4,963	2,714	514	1,735	1·8	0·3	1·1	3·2
Northumberland	19,973	11,891	5,138	2,944	2·1	0·9	0·5	3·5
Nottinghamshire	9,436	5,527	1,575	2,334	2·0	0·6	0·8	3·4
Somerset ..	9,544	5,351	1,214	2,979	2·1	0·5	1·2	3·8
West Riding ..	16,501	10,709	3,412	2,380	2·5	0·8	0·6	3·9
East Sussex ..	2,965	1,554	326	1,085	1·6	0·3	1·1	3·0
Total ..	66,090	39,304	12,988	13,798	2·1	0·7	0·7	3·6

TABLE II

(b) 12 YEAR OLDS

Area	Total Number of D.M.F. Teeth	Total of 'D' Teeth	Total of 'M' Teeth	Total of 'F' Teeth	Average Number of 'D' Teeth per Child	Average Number of 'M' Teeth per Child	Average Number of 'F' Teeth per Child	Total of D.M.F. Teeth
Manchester ..	3,023	681	517	1,825	1·0	0·7	2·6	4·2
Middlesex ..	8,982	1,692	708	6,582	0·9	0·4	3·6	4·9
Northumberland	27,256	7,840	5,715	13,701	1·5	1·1	2·6	5·2
Nottinghamshire	11,353	3,676	1,508	6,169	1·6	0·7	2·8	5·1
Somerset ..	13,351	3,502	1,089	8,760	1·4	0·4	3·5	5·3
West Riding ..	26,521	9,378	3,198	13,945	2·0	0·7	3·0	5·7
East Sussex ..	7,942	1,658	535	5,749	1·0	0·3	3·5	4·8
Total ..	98,428	28,427	13,270	56,731	1·5	0·7	3·0	5·2

FIGURE 1

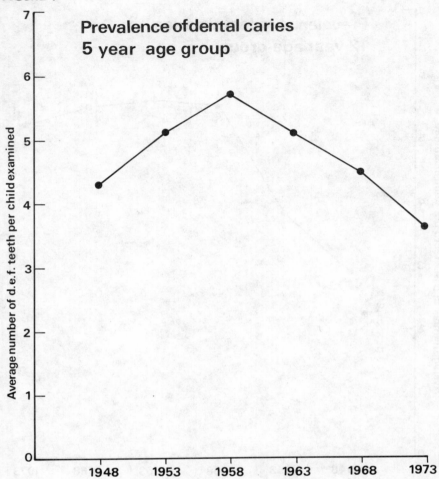

FIGURE 2

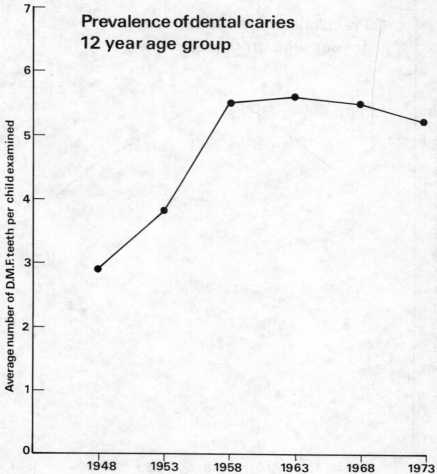

Prevalence of dental caries
12 year age group

FIGURE 3

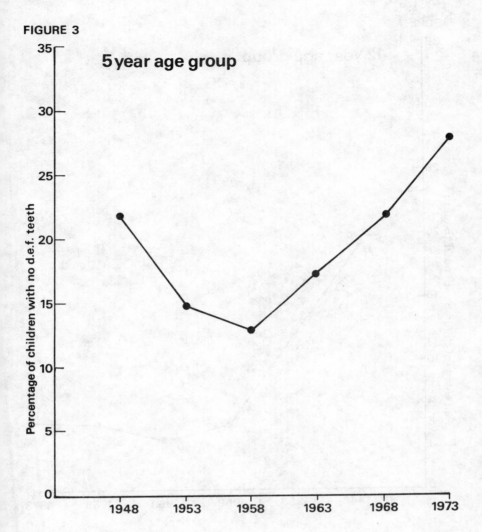

FIGURE 4

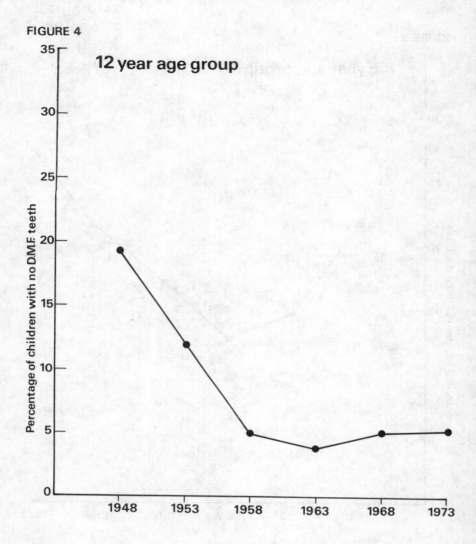

12 year age group

FIGURE 5

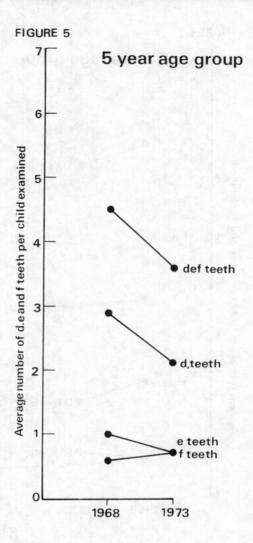

FIGURE 6

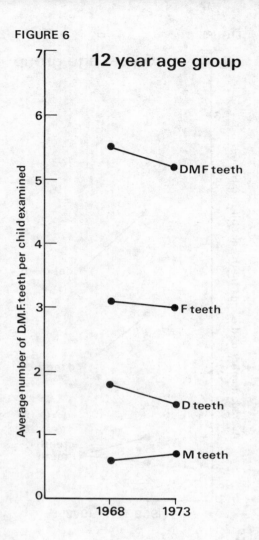

12 year age group

The reduction in the prevalence of caries cannot be ascribed to any particular cause. It is possible that dental health education given over a long period of time is now playing a more effective role and reducing the levels of dental disease. Sugar consumption reached its peak in 1958 when the average sugar consumption (including honey and glucose) per head of population was 122 lbs. Sugar consumption per head of population was 106 lbs in 1938 being reduced to under 80 lbs per head during the war years. In 1948 it was 88 lbs. Whilst it was 118 lbs per head in 1972 the glucose content has increased to 13 lbs as against 7 lbs in 1958 and this may have exerted some benign influence (albeit of a minor nature) on the caries prevalence. The greatest reduction of caries has occurred in very young children and as this group are less liable to have treatment sought for them the benefit is all the more gratifying.

In 1965 a special survey of 15,000 schoolchildren aged 15 years was carried out in 30 local education authorities. It showed that fewer than 2% of the children had received no dental treatment during their school lives from any source. On average both boys and girls had 4 teeth requiring filling, 2 teeth missing or requiring to be extracted and 4 teeth that had been satisfactorily filled. In every region grammar school children had more satisfactorily filled teeth and fewer missing teeth than have secondary modern school pupils (The Department of Education and Science 1972a).

Ratio of School Dentists to School Population and Percentage of Children Treated

Although the number of school dentists almost doubled between 1938 and 1972 from the equivalent of 783 full-time dentists in 1938 to 1,437 in 1972 there was in the early years a decline in the ratio of dentist to children owing to the large increase in the school population and to the extension of dental treatment to all secondary school pupils: there was the equivalent of one full-time school dentist to 5,780 pupils in 1938 and, to about 6,750 in 1953 and to 5,990 in 1972.

In 1972 of the 8·7 million schoolchildren 5 million had 1 routine dental inspection and about half a million were reinspected; 3 million were found to require dental treatment and 1·4 million (48%) received it on average, each child made 2·7 attendances thus, in 1972 43% of the school population were not examined by a school dentist but 1 child in 6 received treatment through the school dental service.

It is however difficult to correlate all statistics relating to the treatment of schoolchildren. The Dental Estimates Board records the number of completed estimates of cost of inspection and of treatment, not the number of individual children. All children are entitled to inspection and treatment every 4 months in the General Dental Service; and an increasing number of children attend the General Dental Service regularly for examination, or examination and treatment if required. In 1972 there were about 6½ million completed estimates in respect of children aged 5–15 years (a proportion of whom no doubt attended independent schools and did not come under the school dental service); the probability is that the number of children actually treated was less than the total number of courses.

It is unfortunate that precise information is not available about the number of school children treated by the General Dental Service. There is need for better communications between the General and School Dental Services and the reorganisation of the National Health Service should provide the potential for improvement.

On all the evidence there is a continuing need for a vigorous school dental service as part of the national health service and working closely with the schools.

APPENDIX A

STATISTICS OF THE SCHOOL HEALTH SERVICE

TABLE I

Staff of the School Health Service as at 31 December 1973

	Medical Officers						Nurses and Health Visitors			Speech Therapists			Audiometricians	Chiropodists	Orthoptists	Physiotherapists	Others (excluding clerical staff)
	Solely School Health Service	Part-time School Health Service/rest of time on Local Health Service	Part-time School Health Service/rest of time as General Practitioner	Part-time School Health Service/rest of time on other medical work	Ophthalmic Specialists	Other Consultants and Specialists	With Health Visitors' Certificate	Without Health Visitors' Certificate	Nurses' Assistants	Senior Speech Therapists	Speech Therapists	Assistant Speech Therapists					
NUMBER:—																	
England Full-time	110	1,114	—	—	4	—	4,058	1,377	275	125	314	11	81	57	15	153	146
Part-time	73	727	837	437	319	240	2,404	1,604	435	26	482	13	78	202	44	294	112
Wales Full-time	3	117	—	—	—	—	421	164	13	8	7	—	3	16	—	3	8
Part-time	2	50	26	22	14	10	82	162	10	2	20	1	24	2	4	6	—
Total Full-time	113	1,231	—	—	4	—	4,479	1,541	288	133	321	11	84	73	15	156	154
Part-time	75	777	863	459	333	250	2,486	1,766	445	28	502	14	102	204	48	300	112
WHOLE-TIME EQUIVALENT:—																	
England	132·5	767·0	93·3	68·4	64·6	22·4	1,636·1	1,604·4	355·0	136·1	484·1	14·6	119·2	55·6	26·8	245·7	192·4
Wales	3·7	63·2	4·2	7·8	1·7	0·8	109·0	110·5	13·8	7·5	14·8	0·8	5·9	1·1	1·4	4·6	8·0
Total	136·2	830·2	97·5	76·2	66·3	23·2	1,745·1	1,714·9	368·8	143·6	498·9	15·4	125·1	56·7	28·2	250·3	200·4

49

TABLE II

Staff of the School Health Service—Child Guidance and School Psychological Service as at 31 December 1973

	Psychiatrists		Educational Psychologists		Social Workers		Psycho-therapists	Remedial Teachers	Others (excluding clerical staff)
	Employed by the local education authority	Employed under arrangements with Hospital Authority	Employed in Child Guidance Clinics	Employed in the School Psychological service	Qualified	Unqualified			
NUMBER:—									
England Full-time	21	30		603	297	51	36	485	67
Part-time	95	254		100	206	26	80	545	30
Wales Full-time	1	—		36	20	3	—	95	1
Part-time	11	24		3	8	3	—	37	2
Total Full-time	22	30		639	317	54	36	580	68
Part-time	106	278		103	214	29	80	582	32
Whole-time equivalent:—									
England	46·9	116·0	238·0	407·3	400·0	58·6	79·0	705·7	78·9
Wales	4·5	4·4	9·1	28·0	22·2	4·5	—	113·0	2·0
Total	51·4	120·4	247·1	435·3	422·2	63·1	79·0	818·7	80·9

TABLE III

MEDICAL INSPECTIONS

	Number of pupils (1) on the registers of maintained primary and secondary schools (including nursery and special schools) in January 1974	Number of pupils inspected during the year ended 31 December 1973	
		At periodic inspections	At special and re-inspections
England	8,568,976 (2)	1,459,085	1,086,936
Wales	549,702 (2)	77,826	56,539
Total	9,118,678	1,536,911	1,143,475

(1) Full-time pupils and part-time pupils aged under 5 years.
(2) These figures were derived from the returns made on Forms 7 (Schools) 7M and 11 (Schools).

TABLE IV

NUMBER OF CERTAIN DEFECTS KNOWN TO HAVE RECEIVED TREATMENT BY THE AUTHORITY OR OTHERWISE, HOWEVER THEY WERE BROUGHT TO LOCAL EDUCATION AUTHORITIES' NOTICE, I.E. WHETHER BY PERIODIC INSPECTION, SPECIAL INSPECTION OR OTHERWISE, DURING 1973

	Number of defects treated, or under treatment during the year 1973		
	England	Wales	Total
DISEASES OF THE SKIN:			
Ringworm—scalp	336	7	343
Ringworm—body	538	14	552
Scabies	11,376	181	11,557
Impetigo	5,810	104	5,914
Other skin diseases	130,309	2,060	132,369
EYE DISEASES: DEFECTIVE VISION AND SQUINT:			
External and other (excluding errors of refraction and squint)	23,101	2,598	25,699
Errors of refraction and squint	343,263	19,626	362,889
Number of pupils for whom spectacles were prescribed	137,659	9,196	146,855
DEFECTS OF EAR:			
Total number of pupils still on registers of schools at 31 December 1973 known to have been provided with hearing aids:—			
a. during the calendar year 1973	2,320	113	2,433
b. in previous years	15,150	749	15,899
CONVALESCENT TREATMENT:			
Number of pupils who received convalescent treatment under School Health Service arrangements.	6,751	—	6,751
MINOR AILMENTS:			
Number of pupils with minor ailments	284,426	3,064	287,490

51

TABLE V

NUMBER OF CHILDREN KNOWN TO HAVE RECEIVED TREATMENT UNDER CHILD
GUIDANCE ARRANGEMENTS DURING THE YEAR 1973

	Number of clinics	Number of pupils treated
England ..	400	75,775
Wales ..	24	3,490
Total	424	79,265

TABLE VI

NUMBER OF CHILDREN KNOWN TO HAVE RECEIVED TREATMENT UNDER SPEECH
THERAPY ARRANGEMENTS DURING THE YEAR 1973

	Number of clinics	Number of pupils treated
England ..	1,494	104,082
Wales ..	116	5,546
Total	1,610	109,628

TABLE VII

UNCLEANLINESS AND VERMINOUS CONDITIONS FOUND DURING THE YEAR 1973

	Total number of examinations of pupils in schools by School Nurses or other authorised persons	Total number of individual pupils found to be infested	Number of individual pupils in respect of whom were issued:—	
			Cleansing Notices under Section 54(2) of the Education Act 1944	Cleansing Orders under Section 54(3) of the Education Act 1944
England	12,019,813	238,055	45,435	4,645
Wales	813,488	17,700	4,888	73
Total	12,833,301	255,755	50,323	4,718

TABLE VIII

DEATHS BY CAUSE AT AGES UNDER 15 YEARS DURING THE YEAR ENDED 31 DECEMBER 1973

ENGLAND AND WALES

Causes of Death	Under 5 years of age		5–14 years of age		Total		Total male and female
	Male	Female	Male	Female	Male	Female	
1. Enteritis and other diarrhoeal diseases	181	149	5	3	186	152	338
2. Tuberculosis of respiratory system	—	—	—	1	—	1	1
3. Other tuberculosis, including late effects	3	—	3	3	6	3	9
4. Diphtheria	—	—	—	—	—	—	—
5. Whooping cough . .	2	—	—	—	2	—	2
6. Meningococcal infection . .	79	58	7	10	86	68	154
7. Acute poliomyelitis	—	—	—	—	—	—	—
8. Measles	7	8	5	8	12	16	28
9. Syphilis and its sequelae	1	—	—	1	1	1	2
10. All other infective and parasitic diseases . .	94	51	19	20	113	71	184
11. Malignant neoplasms of the stomach . .	—	—	—	—	—	—	—
12. Trachea, bronchus and lung	—	—	1	1	1	1	2
13. Breast	—	—	—	—	—	—	—
14. Cervix uteri and other uterus . .	—	—	—	—	—	—	—
15. Leukaemia, . . aleukaemia . .	67	49	107	65	174	114	288
16. Other malignant neoplasms . .	86	55	128	61	214	116	330
17. Diabetes mellitus . .	2	5	4	9	6	14	20
18. Hypertensive disease	—	1	—	—	—	1	1
19. Ischaemic heart disease	2	—	1	1	3	1	4
20. Other forms of heart disease . .	24	25	32	9	56	34	90
21. Cerebrovascular disease	20	12	25	12	45	24	69
22. Other circulatory diseases	13	9	2	2	15	11	26
23. Influenza	6	5	4	6	10	11	21
24. Pneumonia . .	693	495	55	52	748	547	1,295
25. Bronchitis, all forms	339	239	6	9	345	248	593
26. Other diseases of respiratory system	155	88	35	17	190	105	295
27. Peptic ulcer . .	3	1	—	1	3	2	5
28. Other diseases of digestive system . .	149	95	30	15	179	110	289
29. Nephritis and nephrosis	12	10	6	14	18	24	42
30. Hyperplasia of prostate	—	—	—	—	—	—	—
31. Complications of pregnancy, childbirth and the puerperium	—	—	—	—	—	—	—
32. Congenital anomalies	1,516	1,426	137	116	1,653	1.542	3,195

continued on page 54

53

TABLE VIII—*continued*

Causes of Death	Under 5 years of age		5–14 years of age		Total		Total male and female
	Male	Female	Male	Female	Male	Female	
33. Other defined and ill-defined diseases	3,797	2,593	254	199	4,051	2,792	6,843
34. Motor vehicle accidents	128	65	350	174	478	239	717
35. All other accidents	360	228	245	74	605	302	907
36. Suicide and self-inflicted injuries ..	—	—	3	4	3	4	7
37. All other external causes	63	37	30	16	93	53	146
All causes	7,802	5,704	1,494	903	9,296	6,607	15,903

TABLE IX

NET EXPENDITURE OF LOCAL EDUCATION AUTHORITIES ON THE SCHOOL HEALTH SERVICE FOR THE FINANCIAL YEAR 1ST APRIL 1972— 31ST MARCH 1973

	Net expenditure to be met from grants and rates (excluding loan charges and capital expenditure from revenue) (£000)
England ..	36,022
Wales	2,394
Total	38,416

TABLE X

NUMBERS OF CORRECTED NOTIFICATIONS OF INFECTIOUS DISEASES AMONG CHILDREN UNDER 15 DURING THE YEAR ENDED 31 DECEMBER 1973

ENGLAND AND WALES

	Scarlet Fever		Whooping Cough		Acute Poliomyelitis				Measles		Diphtheria		Dysentery	
					Paralytic		Non-paralytic							
	M	F	M	F	M	F	M	F	M	F	M	F	M	F
Under 5 years	1,709	1,600	723	742	2	—	—	—	38,282	35,992	—	1	1,491	1,206
5–14 years ..	3,881	3,895	439	471	—	2	—	—	38,042	36,311	1	—	1,126	975
Total ..	5,590	5,495	1,162	1,213	2	2	—	—	76,324	72,303	1	1	2,617	2,181

	Smallpox		Acute Encephalitis				Enteric or typhoid fever		Paratyphoid fever		Tuberculosis (all forms)		Acute meningitis		Food poisoning	
			Infective		Post-infectious											
	M	F	M	F	M	F	M	F	M	F	M	F	M	F	M	F
Under 5 years	—	—	9	9	13	8	8	7	6	5	212	170	565	410	719	628
5–14 years	—	—	23	12	19	10	29	20	4	5	395	361	373	220	494	493
Total	—	—	32	21	32	18	37	27	10	10	607	531	938	630	1,213	1,121

APPENDIX B

STATISTICS OF THE SCHOOL DENTAL SERVICE

TABLE I

STAFF OF THE SCHOOL DENTAL SERVICE AS AT 31 DECEMBER 1973

	Dental Officers	Dental Auxiliaries	Dental Surgery Assistants	Dental Hygienists	Dental Technicians	Dental Health Education Personnel	Clerical Assistants
NUMBER:							
England	1,885	244	2,313	19	125	32	171
Wales	136	15	134	—	4	4	18
Total	2,021	259	2,447	19	129	36	189
WHOLE-TIME EQUIVALENT:							
England	1475·7	203·4	1849·7	15·4	100·1	16·8	125·8
Wales	117·5	15·0	119·2	—	4·0	2·4	12·5
Total	1593·2	218·4	1968·9	15·4	104·1	19·2	138·3

56

TABLE II

DENTAL INSPECTION AND TREATMENT DURING THE YEAR ENDED 31 DECEMBER 1973

(A) NUMBER OF PUPILS

Number of pupils on registers in January 1974 = (England = 8,568,976; Wales = 549,702)

	First inspection			Number found to require treatment	Number offered treatment	Number actually treated	% age of pupils found to require treatment who received it	Number of pupils re-inspected at School or Clinic	Number of re-inspected pupils found to require treatment	Attendances made by pupils for treatment
	At school	At clinic	Total							
England	4,028,317	794,317	4,822,634	2,577,016	2,239,992	1,350,095	52·4	491,288	294,755	3,656,439
Wales	225,034	58,928	283,962	164,761	155,942	93,034	56·5	26,110	16,371	249,145
Total	4,253,351	853,245	5,106,596	2,741,777	2,395,934	1,443,129	52·6	517,398	311,126	3,905,584

57

TABLE II—*continued*

(B) Dental Treatment (other than Orthodontic Treatment—see Table II(c))—during the year ended 31 December 1973

	Sessions devoted to			Number of fillings		Number of teeth filled		Number of extractions		Teeth otherwise conserved
	Treatment	Inspection	Dental Health Education	Permanent teeth	Deciduous teeth	Permanent teeth	Deciduous teeth	Permanent teeth	Deciduous teeth	
England	576,281	34,487	14,163	2,192,974	1,021,992	1,842,291	911,252	284,780	775,422	155,603
Wales	42,772	2,419	933	147,475	60,726	120,260	52,928	23,929	53,000	16,204
Total	619,053	36,906	15,096	2,340,449	1,082,718	1,962,551	964,180	308,709	828,422	171,807

	Crowns	Inlays	Teeth root filled	Dentures		Number of pupils X-rayed	Prophylaxis	Number of general anaesthetics administered by	
				Number of pupils supplied with dentures	Number of dentures supplied			Dental Officers	Medical Practitioners
England	8,421	628	10,853	6,037	7,538	135,156	451,029	74,963	219,807
Wales	594	76	1,333	515	623	4,903	25,909	2,779	20,573
Total	9,015	704	12,186	6,552	8,161	140,059	476,938	77,742	240,380

58

TABLE II—continued

(c) Orthodontic Treatment during the year ended 31 December 1973

	Number of cases			Number of appliances fitted		Number of pupils referred to Hospital Consultants
	Commenced during the year	Completed during the year	Discontinued during the year	Removable	Fixed	
England	25,504	18,615	2,884	40,871	2,569	5,636
Wales	1,492	680	95	1,813	204	1,195
Total	26,996	19,295	2,979	42,684	2,773	6,831

TABLE III

DENTAL ATTENDANCE AND TREATMENT BY AGE GROUPS DURING THE YEAR ENDED 31 DECEMBER 1973

	Ages 5–9		Ages 10–14		Ages 15 and over		Total		Total England and Wales
	England	Wales	England	Wales	England	Wales	England	Wales	
Number of first visits (i.e. pupils treated)	657,988	47,502	567,324	36,762	124,783	8,770	1,350,095	93,034	1,443,129
Subsequent visits	915,403	66,214	1,103,644	69,602	280,381	20,295	2,299,428	156,111	2,455,539
Total visits	1,573,391	113,716	1,670,968	106,364	405,164	29,065	3,649,523	249,145	3,898,668
Additional courses of treatment commenced	89,805	4,173	75,811	3,265	18,672	968	184,288	8,406	192,694
Fillings in permanent teeth	537,297	36,057	1,257,575	82,057	398,102	29,361	2,192,974	147,475	2,340,449
Fillings in deciduous teeth	918,311	55,189	103,681	5,537	—	—	1,021,992	60,726	1,082,718
Permanent teeth filled	427,857	26,584	1,068,022	68,724	346,412	24,952	1,842,291	120,260	1,902,551
Deciduous teeth filled	818,640	48,140	92,612	6,788	—	—	911,252	52,928	964,180
Permanent teeth extracted	43,961	3,452	191,983	15,664	48,836	4,813	284,780	23,929	308,709
Deciduous teeth extracted	572,004	40,335	203,418	12,665	—	—	775,422	53,000	828,422
General anaesthetics	181,709	14,461	100,383	7,665	12,678	1,226	294,770	23,352	318,122
Emergencies (treatment)	98,029	7,628	63,188	4,782	15,140	1,236	176,357	13,646	190,003
Courses of treatment completed	—	—	—	—	—	—	1,227,315	72,188	1,299,503

TABLE IV

PROSTHETICS 1973 (BY AGE GROUPS)

		Ages 5–9	Ages 10–14	Ages 15 and over	Total
Pupils supplied with full dentures for the first time	England	24	79	167	270
	Wales	—	12	41	53
	Total	24	91	208	323
Pupils supplied with other dentures for the first time	England	364	3,334	2,069	5,767
	Wales	19	244	199	462
	Total	383	3,578	2,268	6,229
Number of dentures supplied (first or subsequent time)	England	478	4,182	2,878	7,538
	Wales	20	292	311	623
	Total	498	4,474	3,189	8,161

61

TABLE V

ANALYSIS OF DUTIES OF DENTAL OFFICERS, DENTAL AUXILIARIES AND DENTAL HYGIENISTS FOR THE YEAR ENDED 31 DECEMBER 1973

i. Dental Officers

	Number of Officers	Total full-time equivalent inclusive of extra paid sessions worked		
		Administrative duties	Clinical duties	
			School Service	M & CW Service
PSDO	175	72·9	92·0	9·3
Dental Officers (employed on salary basis)	1,234	18·6	1126·0	66·3
Dental Officers (employed on sessional basis) ..	612	—	197·9	11·4
Total	2,021	91·5	1415·9	87·0

ii. Dental Auxiliaries and Dental Hygienists

	Number of Officers	Full-time equivalent	
		School Service	M & CW Service
Dental Auxiliaries	259	197·9	20·5
Dental Hygienists	19	12·9	2·5

APPENDIX C

HANDICAPPED PUPILS REQUIRING AND RECEIVING EDUCATION IN SPECIAL SCHOOLS APPROVED UNDER SECTION 9(5) OF THE EDUCATION ACT, 1944; RECEIVING EDUCATION IN INDEPENDENT SCHOOLS, IN SPECIAL CLASSES AND UNITS; BOARDED IN HOMES AND RECEIVING EDUCATION IN ACCORDANCE WITH SECTION 56 OF THE EDUCATION ACT

ENGLAND AND WALES

		Blind	Partially Sighted	Deaf	Partially Hearing	Physically Handicapped	Delicate	Maladjusted	E.S.N. and Autistic	Epileptic	Suffering from Speech defects	Total
1.	During the year ending 31st December, 1973 number of handicapped pupils who were:—											
A.	Newly assessed as needing special educational treatment at special schools or in boarding homes	138	300	279	565	1,885	1,603	4,043	13,639	161	158	22,771
B.	Newly placed in special schools (other than hospital special schools) or boarding homes	124	293	338	599	1,810	1,667	3,047	13,841	173	162	22,054
2.	In January, 1974 number of handicapped children who were:—											
A.	Requiring places in special schools (i) Day	11	80	54	158	534	254	397	7,537	6	18	9,049
	(ii) Boarding	89	93	58	110	198	344	1,893	1,205	58	58	4,106
B.	On the registers of maintained special schools including attached Units and Hospital Special Schools. (i) Day	70	1,268	1,529	1,615	7,668	3,675	3,795	78,208	486	625	98,939
	(ii) Boarding	235	443	467	443	1,510	1,730	3,033	9,953	86	44	17,944
C.	On the registers of non-maintained special schools including attached Units and Hospital Special Schools. (i) Day	37	56	231	98	410	—	12	448	9	4	1,305
	(ii) Boarding	788	453	1,275	516	1,268	525	1,037	1,241	466	90	7,659
D.	On the registers of independent schools under arrangements made by local education authorities	15	15	258	127	673	207	3,575	1,214	14	35	6,133
E.	Boarded in Homes and not already included in 2B, C or D above	1	1	—	—	7	113	626	70	—	1	819
F.	Being educated under arrangements (i) in hospitals	—	5	—	—	187	38	163	545	4	6	948
	made in accordance with Section 56 (ii) in other groups	5	6	37	69	464	31	967	648	11	42	2,280
	of the Education Act, 1944. (iii) at home	21	7	8	8	766	365	773	332	42	4	2,326
G.	Being educated in special classes in ordinary schools (assume all day)	2	112	106	2,028	268	143	1,276	9,851	72	474	14,332
	Total receiving special educational treatment and awaiting places	1,274	2,539	4,023	5,172	13,953	7,425	17,547	111,252	1,254	1,401	165,840

REFERENCES

Adelstein, A. M. and Scully, J. (1967). Brit. med. J. pp. 334–338.

Binnie, H. L. (1971). Brit. med. J. 3. 354.

Board of Education (1910a). Annual Report for 1908 of the Chief Medical Officer. London. HMSO, p. 4.

Board of Education (1910b). Annual Report for 1908 of the Chief Medical Officer. London. HMSO. p. 112.

Board of Education (1910c). Annual Report for 1908 of the Chief Medical Officer. London. HMSO. pp. 153, 154.

Board of Education (1910d). Annual Report for 1908 of the Chief Medical Officer. London. HMSO. pp. 120–125.

Board of Education (1910e). Annual Report for 1908 of the Chief Medical Officer. London. HMSO. p. 125.

Board of Education (1910f). Annual Report for 1909 of the Chief Medical Officer. London. HMSO pp. 153, 154–157, 208–210.

Board of Education (1911). Annual Report for 1910 of the Chief Medical Officer. London. HMSO. p. 195.

Board of Education (1914a). Annual Report for 1913 of the Chief Medical Officer. London. HMSO. p. 89.

Board of Education (1914b). Annual Report for 1913 of the Chief Medical Officer. London. HMSO. p. 237.

Board of Education (1918). Annual Report for 1917 of the Chief Medical Officer. London. HMSO. p. 166.

Board of Education (1920). Annual Report for 1919 of the Chief Medical Officer. London. HMSO. pp. 127–128.

Board of Education (1921a) Annual Report for 1920 of the Chief Medical Officer. London. HMSO. pp. 109–110.

Board of Education (1921b). Annual Report for 1920 of the Chief Medical Officer. London. HMSO. pp. 3–4.

Board of Education (1927a). Annual Report for 1926 of the Chief Medical Officer. London. HMSO. p. 61.

Board of Education (1927b). Annual Report for 1926 of the Chief Medical Officer. London. HMSO. p. 133.

Board of Education (1928a). Annual Report for 1927 of the Chief Medical Officer. London. HMSO. pp. 153–154.

Board of Education (1928b). Annual Report for 1927 of the Chief Medical Officer. London. HMSO. p. 31.

Board of Education (1931a). Annual Report for 1930 of the Chief Medical Officer. London. HMSO. p. 20.

Board of Education (1931b). Annual Report for 1930 of the Chief Medical Officer. London. HMSO. p. 108.

Board of Education (1932). Annual Report for 1931 of the Chief Medical Officer. London. HMSO. pp. 80–81.

Board of Education (1933). Annual Report for 1932 of the Chief Medical Officer. London. HMSO. p. 32.

Board of Education (1938). Report of the Committee of Inquiry into the Problems relating to Children with Defective Hearing. London. HMSO.

Colley, J. R. T., Douglas, J. W. B. and Reid, D. D. (1973). Brit. med. J. 3, 195–198.

Department of Education and Science (1964). The Health of the School Child 1962–63 London, HMSO, pp. 64–68.

Department of Education and Science (1966a). The Health of the School Child 1964–65 London, HMSO, pp. 35, 36, 37.

Department of Education and Science (1966b). The Health of the School Child 1964–65 London, HMSO, p. 52.

Department of Education and Science (1968a). The Education of Deaf Children, The Possible Place of Finger Spelling and Signing, London, HMSO, pp. 95, 106.

Department of Education and Science (1968b). A Handbook of Health Education, London, HMSO. Introduction p. vii.

Department of Education and Science (1969a). The Health of the School Child 1966–68. London, HMSO, p. 40.

Department of Education and Science (1969b). The Health of the School Child 1966–68 London, HMSO pp. 67–69.

Department of Education and Science (1971a). Circular No. 6/71. Education of Autistic Children. London. HMSO.

Department of Education and Science (1971b). Slow Learners in Secondary Schools. Education Survey No. 15. London. HMSO.

Department of Education and Science (1972a). The Health of the School Child for 1969–70 London, HMSO, p. 101.

Department of Education and Science (1972b). The Health of the School Child for 1969–70 London, HMSO, pp. 42, 50, 108, 110, 122.

Department of Education and Science (1972c). The Health of the School Child for 1969–70 London, HMSO, pp. 50–54.

Department of Education and Science (1972d). The Education of Visually Handicapped Children, London, HMSO, pp. 43, 109.

Department of Education and Science (1972e). The Health of the School Child, 1969–70 London, HMSO, pp. 72–78.

Department of Education and Science (1972f). Speech Therapy Services Report. London, HMSO, para. 7.46, p. 85.

Department of Education and Science (1972g). The Health of the School Child, 1969–70. London. HMSO. p. 122.

Department of Education and Science (1972h). Drugs and the Schools. London, HMSO.

Department of Education and Science (1972i). The Education of Visually Handicapped Children, London, HMSO, p. 108.

Department of Education and Science (1972j). The Health of the School Child, 1969–70 London, HMSO, p. 111.

Department of Health and Social Security (1971). Circular No. CMO 12/71. London, HMSO.

Department of Health and Social Security (1973a). Working Party on Collaboration between the NHS and London Government Report on its activities to the end of 1972. London, HMSO. p. 64.

Department of Health and Social Security (1973b). Working Party on Collaboration between the NHS and Local Government Report on its activities to the end of 1972. London, HMSO. p. 95.

Department of Health and Social Security (1973c). Annual Report for 1972. London, HMSO. pp. 117 and 122.

Field, E., Hammond, W. H. and Tizard, J. (1971). Thirteen-year-old Approved School Boys in 1962. London, HMSO.

Fine, S. R. (1968). Blind and Partially-sighted Children. Education Survey No. 4, London, HMSO.

Home Office (1970a). Children in Care in England and Wales. March, 1970. London, HMSO.

Home Office (1970b). Report on the Work of the Children's Department 1967–69. London, HMSO.

Kanner, L. (1943). Autistic Disturbance of Affective Content. *Nerv. Child.*, 2, 217.

Ministry of Education (1949). The Health of the School Child for 1946–47. London, HMSO, p. 68.

Ministry of Education (1952). The Health of the School Child for 1950–51. London, HMSO, pp. 101–124.

Ministry of Education (1954). The Health of the School Child for 1952–53. London, HMSO, pp. 45–46.

Ministry of Education (1955a). Report of the Committee on Maladjusted Children. London, HMSO.

Ministry of Education (1955b). Report of the Committee on Maladjusted Children. London, HMSO, pp. 71 and 83.

Ministry of Education (1960). The Health of the School Child for 1958–59. London, HMSO, p. 39.

Ministry of Education (1964). Slow Learners at School. Pamphlet No. 46. London, HMSO.

Mitchell, R. G. (1973). *Lancet*. 1. 651–656.

Registrar General (1973a). Statistical Review of England and Wales for 1971. Part II. Tables. Population. London, HMSO.

Registrar General (1973b). Statistical Review of England and Wales for 1971. Part I, Tables. Medical. London, HMSO.

Reid, M. (1971). Audiological Services for Children. *Hearing*. Vol. 26, No. 2, pp. 36–40.

Report of the Interdepartmental Committee on the Medical Inspection and Feeding of Children attending Public Elementary Schools (1905).

Report of the Interdepartmental Committee on Physical Deterioration (1904).

Report of the Royal Commission on Physical Training in Scotland (1903).

Rutter, M., Tizard, J. and Whitmore, K. (1970). Education, Health and Behaviour. London. pp. 285, 292, 298, 314.

Smith, C. S. (1971). *Well Being*. Vol. 2, No. 2. West Riding of Yorkshire Health Department.

Smith, J. M. (1961). *Brit. med. J.*, 1. 711.

United Kingdom Dental Mission (1950). New Zealand School Dental Nurses. Report London. HMSO.

United Kingdom Mission (1953). Fluoridation of Domestic Water Supplies in North America as a Means of Controlling Dental Caries. Report. London. HMSO.

Wallas, Graham (1940). Men and Ideas. London. p. 81.

Wing, J. K., O'Connor, N. and Lotter, V. (1967). *Brit. med. J.*, 3. 389–392.

Printed in England for Her Majesty's Stationery Office by McCorquodale Printers Ltd. London
HM 3309   Dd 289777   K41   8/75   McC3309